JUMBLE®
Symphony

An Orchestra of Perplexing Puzzles!

Jeff Knurek,
David L. Hoyt,
Henri Arnold,
and Bob Lee

TRIUMPH
BOOKS

This book is available in quantity at special discounts
for your group or organization.

For further information, contact:

Triumph Books LLC
814 North Franklin Street
Chicago, Illinois 60610
Phone: (312) 337-0747
www.triumphbooks.com

Printed in U.S.A.

ISBN: 978-1-62937-131-3

Design by Sue Knopf

Contents

JUMBLE® Symphony

Classic Puzzles

PUZZLE 1

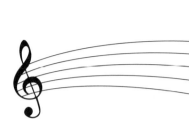

Unscramble these four Jumbles, one letter to each square, to form four ordinary words.

DYGUP

PUMBY

MIOGES

YIFNER

WHAT IT WAS WHEN THE DOCTOR SAID, "THIS WON'T HURT."

Now arrange the circled letters to form the surprise answer, as suggested by the above cartoon.

Print answer here AN "☐.☐," ☐☐☐☐☐☐☐☐

2

JUMBLE®

Unscramble these four Jumbles, one letter to each square, to form four ordinary words.

AMMIX

FEWAR

AMPIGE

HARSHT

THE WAITER FINALLY COMES TO THIS.

Now arrange the circled letters to form the surprise answer, as suggested by the above cartoon.

Print answer here ⟨◯◯◯⟩ WHO ⟨◯◯◯◯◯◯⟩

3

JUMBLE®

Unscramble these four Jumbles, one letter to each square, to form four ordinary words.

ORXAB

RAFIE

FENTOM

WARBOR

HE WAS THE TYPE OF MAN SOME WOMEN TAKE TO — AND ALSO THIS.

Now arrange the circled letters to form the surprise answer, as suggested by the above cartoon.

Print answer here

JUMBLE®

Unscramble these four Jumbles, one letter to each square, to form four ordinary words.

TAING
◯◯◯◯◯

URUGA
◯◯◯◯◯

KRODEF
◯◯◯◯◯◯

CHINTS
◯◯◯◯◯◯

WHAT THEY CALLED THE STAR OF THE MONSTER SHOW.

Now arrange the circled letters to form the surprise answer, as suggested by the above cartoon.

Print answer here   A ◯◯◯◯◯ " ◯◯◯◯◯◯ "

JUMBLE.

Unscramble these four Jumbles, one letter to each square, to form four ordinary words.

GOUNY
◯◯◯◯◯

ODITI
◯◯◯◯◯

REDDEG
☐☐☐◯☐◯

LADVAN
◯☐◯◯☐◯

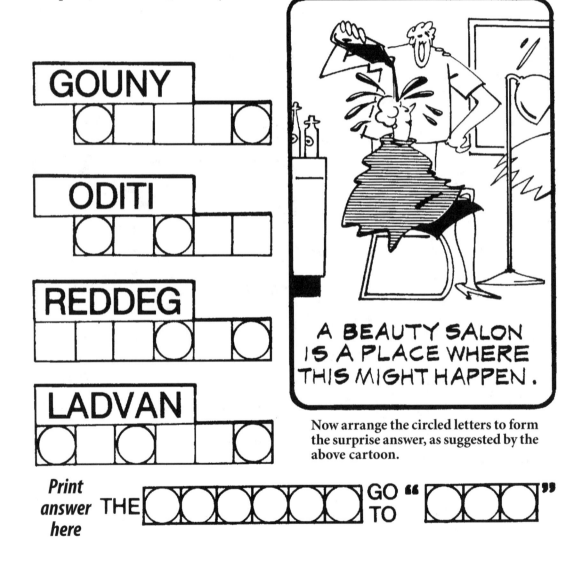

A BEAUTY SALON IS A PLACE WHERE THIS MIGHT HAPPEN.

Now arrange the circled letters to form the surprise answer, as suggested by the above cartoon.

Print answer here

THE ◯◯◯◯◯◯ GO TO " ◯◯◯ "

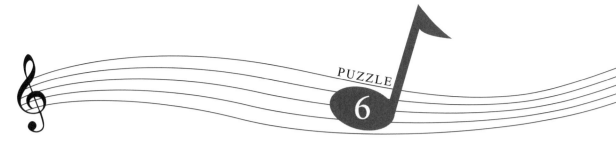

JUMBLE®

Unscramble these four Jumbles, one letter to each square, to form four ordinary words.

WALBY

REGIM

PINKAD

BOLUDE

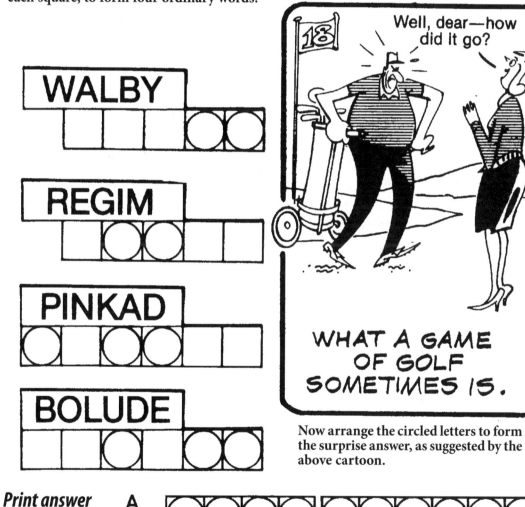

Well, dear—how did it go?

WHAT A GAME OF GOLF SOMETIMES IS.

Now arrange the circled letters to form the surprise answer, as suggested by the above cartoon.

Print answer here

A GOOD ◯◯◯◯◯ ◯◯◯◯◯◯◯

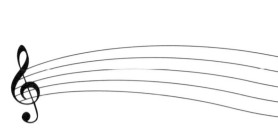

Unscramble these four Jumbles, one letter to each square, to form four ordinary words.

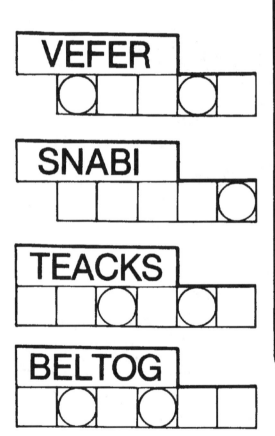

VEFER

SNABI

TEACKS

BELTOG

I've got my retirement all figured out

THE BEST THING TO SAVE FOR OLD AGE.

Now arrange the circled letters to form the surprise answer, as suggested by the above cartoon.

Print answer here

8

JUMBLE®

Unscramble these four Jumbles, one letter to each square, to form four ordinary words.

LYPHS

PYDET

INSLUM

LOUHRY

He had plenty of vigor

And connections!

WHAT YOU HAVE TO HAVE LOTS OF IN ORDER TO OPEN UP THE DOOR TO SUCCESS.

Now arrange the circled letters to form the surprise answer, as suggested by the above cartoon.

Print answer here ⬡⬡⬡⬡ & ⬡⬡⬡⬡

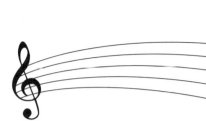

Unscramble these four Jumbles, one letter to each square, to form four ordinary words.

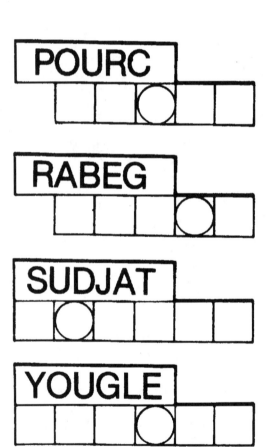

POURC

RABEG

SUDJAT

YOUGLE

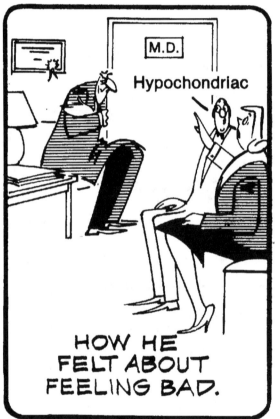

M.D.

Hypochondriac

HOW HE FELT ABOUT FEELING BAD.

Now arrange the circled letters to form the surprise answer, as suggested by the above cartoon.

Print answer here

JUMBLE®

Unscramble these four Jumbles, one letter to each square, to form four ordinary words.

DUGIE

NASDY

TINNEY

FRYLUR

WHAT THE UNHAPPY PIG WAS.

Now arrange the circled letters to form the surprise answer, as suggested by the above cartoon.

Print answer here " ◯◯◯ - ◯◯◯◯◯ - ◯◯◯ "

11

JUMBLE®

Unscramble these four Jumbles, one letter to each square, to form four ordinary words.

RAWLD

HEGIT

TICPED

ASANUE

Wait'll the gang hears about THIS!

IF YOU'RE GOING TO ACT LIKE A SKUNK JUST MAKE SURE THAT NOBODY DOES THIS.

Now arrange the circled letters to form the surprise answer, as suggested by the above cartoon.

Print answer here ◯◯◯◯ ◯◯◯◯ OF IT

JUMBLE®

Unscramble these four Jumbles, one letter to each square, to form four ordinary words.

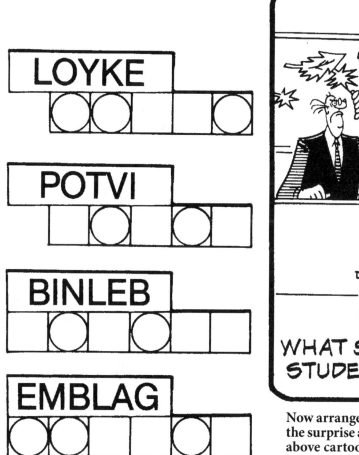

LOYKE

POTVI

BINLEB

EMBLAG

Kid brother was crying all night...

WHAT SOME COLLEGE STUDENTS MAJOR IN.

Now arrange the circled letters to form the surprise answer, as suggested by the above cartoon.

Print answer here " ⃝⃝⃝⃝⃝ - ⃝⃝⃝⃝⃝ "

JUMBLE®

Unscramble these four Jumbles, one letter to
each square, to form four ordinary words.

VOGEL

FELCT

TUSACC

DOAFER

Pay you later

WHAT THE RUNNER'S
DIET CONSISTED
OF, NATURALLY.

Now arrange the circled letters to form
the surprise answer, as suggested by the
above cartoon.

Print answer here

JUMBLE®

Unscramble these four Jumbles, one letter to
each square, to form four ordinary words.

THABI

SUAPE

RAHBOR

DRENGE

We're
the
best!

WHAT THOSE
SNOBBISH MEMBERS
OF THE HORSEY SET
THOUGHT THEY WERE.

Now arrange the circled letters to form
the surprise answer, as suggested by the
above cartoon.

**Print answer
here** A

JUMBLE®

Unscramble these four Jumbles, one letter to each square, to form four ordinary words.

TYSOO

NOAKE

HARTER

MURTES

We've found them all!

WHAT YOU MIGHT GET FROM ASTRONOMERS.

Now arrange the circled letters to form the surprise answer, as suggested by the above cartoon.

Print answer here " ⬡⬡ ⬡⬡⬡ ⬡⬡⬡⬡⬡ "

JUMBLE®

Unscramble these four Jumbles, one letter to each square, to form four ordinary words.

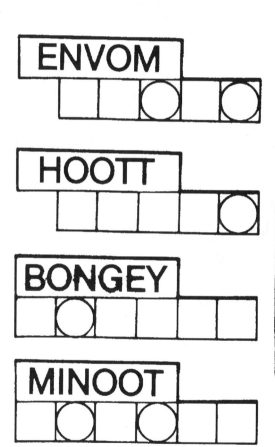

ENVOM

HOOTT

BONGEY

MINOOT

HOW THOSE FOLKS WHO ENJOYED EATING GRITS SANG.

Now arrange the circled letters to form the surprise answer, as suggested by the above cartoon.

Print answer here IN "  "

17

JUMBLE®

Unscramble these four Jumbles, one letter to
each square, to form four ordinary words.

ORPEN

KYSHU

KROMES

VEELEN

WHAT DO YOU THINK
OF THAT POET?

Now arrange the circled letters to form
the surprise answer, as suggested by the
above cartoon.

*Print answer
here* I'VE ⬡⬡⬡⬡⬡ " ⬡⬡⬡⬡⬡⬡ "

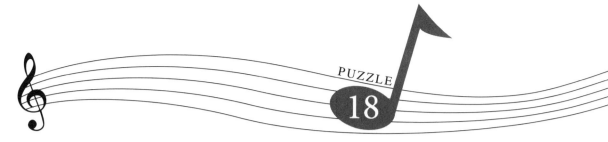

JUMBLE®

Unscramble these four Jumbles, one letter to
each square, to form four ordinary words.

USEAT

DARNB

YALTER

UNSOIC

WHAT HE DID
WHEN SHE ASKED HIM
TO BUY HER THAT
EXPENSIVE PERFUME.

Now arrange the circled letters to form
the surprise answer, as suggested by the
above cartoon.

Print answer here HE " ☐ - ☐☐☐☐☐☐☐ "

JUMBLE®

Unscramble these four Jumbles, one letter to each square, to form four ordinary words.

PARVO

RAMEF

MURBEN

LUSTYS

WHY THEY CALLED FOR THE CHIMNEY SWEEP.

Now arrange the circled letters to form the surprise answer, as suggested by the above cartoon.

Print answer here IT WAS THE " ◯◯◯◯ " ◯◯◯◯◯◯

JUMBLE®

Unscramble these four Jumbles, one letter to each square, to form four ordinary words.

NAUHM

ARBSS

DECLUD

POATTE

It wasn't there yesterday

WHAT HE WAS WHEN HE SAW THAT TREE TRUNK RIGHT IN THE MIDDLE OF THE ROAD.

Now arrange the circled letters to form the surprise answer, as suggested by the above cartoon.

Print answer here "  "

21

JUMBLE®

Unscramble these four Jumbles, one letter to each square, to form four ordinary words.

FOMIT

VENOW

LOPARR

RALFOL

HOW HE FELT AFTER EATING TOO MANY PANCAKES.

Now arrange the circled letters to form the surprise answer, as suggested by the above cartoon.

Print answer here " ◯◯◯◯◯◯ "

JUMBLE®

Unscramble these four Jumbles, one letter to each square, to form four ordinary words.

PIRGE

HUTOM

SPUGMY

REBUPS

WHAT SMALL
SLED DOGS
ARE CALLED.

Now arrange the circled letters to form the surprise answer, as suggested by the above cartoon.

Print answer here " ⬡⬡⬡⬡ " ⬡⬡⬡⬡⬡⬡⬡

JUMBLE®

Unscramble these four Jumbles, one letter to each square, to form four ordinary words.

GLITH

ORRIP

NOCARE

UDDEGI

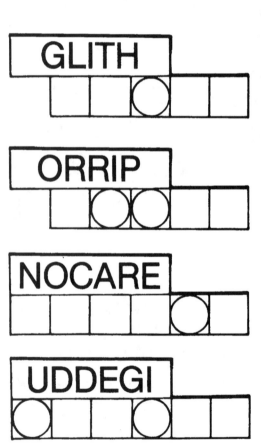

Something's wrong

WHAT THE CARD GAME AT THE OIL FIELD MUST HAVE BEEN.

Now arrange the circled letters to form the surprise answer, as suggested by the above cartoon.

Print answer here "  "

JUMBLE®

Unscramble these four Jumbles, one letter to each square, to form four ordinary words.

EVVAL

KECHE

IBBART

BATERY

HOW THEY GREETED
EACH OTHER AT
THE CARDIOLOGISTS'
ANNUAL SHINDIG.

Now arrange the circled letters to form the surprise answer, as suggested by the above cartoon.

Print answer here

JUMBLE®

Unscramble these four Jumbles, one letter to each square, to form four ordinary words.

RATTI

NEFEC

SPOXEE

RACLIG

WHAT FIREWOOD USED TO BE.

Now arrange the circled letters to form the surprise answer, as suggested by the above cartoon.

Print answer here ⬡⬡⬡⬡ FOR " THE ⬡⬡⬡⬡⬡ "

JUMBLE®

Symphony

Daily Puzzles

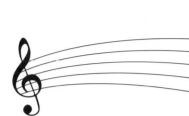

Unscramble these four Jumbles, one letter to each square, to form four ordinary words.

JEECT

VOARS

RECHIP

ASHRIP

TWEET
TWEET

SOUNDS LIKE A FISH WHO THINKS HE'S A BIRD.

Now arrange the circled letters to form the surprise answer, as suggested by the above cartoon.

Print answer here A ☐☐☐☐☐ ON A ☐☐☐☐☐☐

JUMBLE®

Unscramble these four Jumbles, one letter to
each square, to form four ordinary words.

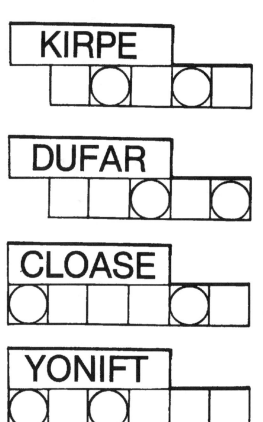

KIRPE

DUFAR

CLOASE

YONIFT

PIZZA

Willpower,
willpower

THE BEST WAY TO
WATCH CALORIES,
IF YOU WANT
TO LOSE WEIGHT.

Now arrange the circled letters to form
the surprise answer, as suggested by the
above cartoon.

Print answer here FROM A ⬭⬭⬭⬭⬭⬭⬭⬭

JUMBLE®

Unscramble these four Jumbles, one letter to
each square, to form four ordinary words.

KOVEE

MASCK

PROWED

HEWPEN

WHAT THE
HELICOPTER
TYCOON DECIDED TO
GET FOR HIMSELF.

Now arrange the circled letters to form
the surprise answer, as suggested by the
above cartoon.

*Print answer
here*

JUMBLE®

Unscramble these four Jumbles, one letter to
each square, to form four ordinary words.

EUQER

SOUDE

NARTTY

SHEERY

WHAT THEY
SAID ABOUT THE
ANGRY GOVERNOR.

Now arrange the circled letters to form
the surprise answer, as suggested by the
above cartoon.

**Print
answer
here**

WHAT " A " ◯◯◯◯◯ " ◯◯ ' ◯ IN !

JUMBLE®

Unscramble these four Jumbles, one letter to each square, to form four ordinary words.

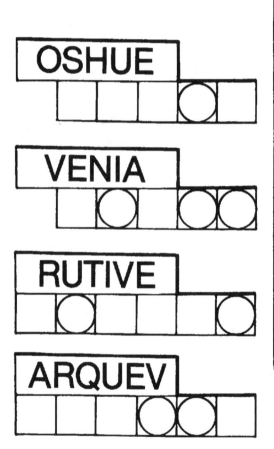

OSHUE

VENIA

RUTIVE

ARQUEV

I have an alibi

WHAT JUNIOR WAS WHEN MOM ACCUSED HIM OF BREAKING HER FAVORITE URN.

Now arrange the circled letters to form the surprise answer, as suggested by the above cartoon.

Print answer here " ☐ - ☐☐☐☐ - ☐☐☐ "

JUMBLE®

Unscramble these four Jumbles, one letter to each square, to form four ordinary words.

OUMID

CHACO

YIPTTS

CINUDE

Aw—drop dead!

WHAT THE HASH SLINGER KNEW HOW TO DO.

Now arrange the circled letters to form the surprise answer, as suggested by the above cartoon.

Print answer here

33

JUMBLE®

Unscramble these four Jumbles, one letter to each square, to form four ordinary words.

NOJIT

CHOAR

GAPOAD

BLAMCY

If you don't give us what we want, it means war!

WHAT "DIPLOMACY" SOMETIMES TURNS OUT TO BE.

Now arrange the circled letters to form the surprise answer, as suggested by the above cartoon.

Print answer here " ◯◯◯ ◯◯◯◯◯◯ "

JUMBLE®

Unscramble these four Jumbles, one letter to each square, to form four ordinary words.

RINDE

CENIE

RAPOUR

UNPOOC

NO VACANCIES

HOW THE HOTEL ROOM CLERK APPEARED.

Now arrange the circled letters to form the surprise answer, as suggested by the above cartoon.

Print answer here " _____ "

35

JUMBLE®

Unscramble these four Jumbles, one letter to each square, to form four ordinary words.

BERPO

YUSUR

SNORGT

TUMONT

HOW HE WORKED HIS WAY "DOWN" IN THE WORLD.

Now arrange the circled letters to form the surprise answer, as suggested by the above cartoon.

Print answer here FROM ⬡⬡⬡⬡⬡⬡⬡ "⬡⬡"

JUMBLE®

Unscramble these four Jumbles, one letter to
each square, to form four ordinary words.

IRQUE

GOBUM

FOLFAY

CHURCO

PRICES REDUCED

DID THE
X-RATED MOVIE
MAKE ANY MONEY?

Now arrange the circled letters to form
the surprise answer, as suggested by the
above cartoon.

Print answer here " ◯◯◯◯ - ◯◯ "

JUMBLE®

Unscramble these four Jumbles, one letter to
each square, to form four ordinary words.

NAWGO

GORPY

UNBOCE

ZARWID

I think I know what to
get Junior for his
next birthday

WHAT BOYS DO WHEN
THEY GROW UP.

Now arrange the circled letters to form
the surprise answer, as suggested by the
above cartoon.

Print answer here ⬡⬡⬡⬡ " ⬡⬡⬡⬡ "

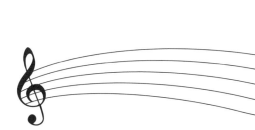

Unscramble these four Jumbles, one letter to each square, to form four ordinary words.

KLAYN

WHAAS

NURYGH

CADETH

Lives from day to day

WHAT SORT OF EXISTENCE DID THAT CRAPSHOOTER LEAD?

Now arrange the circled letters to form the surprise answer, as suggested by the above cartoon.

Print answer here A " ⃝⃝⃝⃝⃝ " ONE

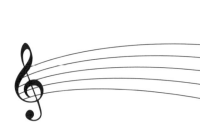

JUMBLE®

Unscramble these four Jumbles, one letter to each square, to form four ordinary words.

KELLN

NYNIF

PRITOM

LENCAG

Lucky to find such a
good place

THERE'S USUALLY
A FINE FOR
PARKING IN ANY
SPOT THAT'S THIS.

Now arrange the circled letters to form the surprise answer, as suggested by the above cartoon.

Print answer here

◯◯◯◯ FOR ◯◯◯◯◯◯◯

JUMBLE®

Unscramble these four Jumbles, one letter to each square, to form four ordinary words.

DYBER

NOOLC

INKANP

SHOPIN

He'll never get anywhere

WHAT A WORKER WHO ALWAYS WATCHES THE CLOCK GENERALLY REMAINS.

Now arrange the circled letters to form the surprise answer, as suggested by the above cartoon.

Print answer here ☐☐☐ OF THE "☐☐☐☐☐"

JUMBLE®

Unscramble these four Jumbles, one letter to
each square, to form four ordinary words.

SEGIN

ROBOD

GONALO

SCUMEL

WHAT A GOOD
BOOK USUALLY IS.

Now arrange the circled letters to form
the surprise answer, as suggested by the
above cartoon.

Print answer " ⬡⬡⬡⬡⬡ " TO ⬡⬡⬡⬡
here

JUMBLE®

Unscramble these four Jumbles, one letter to
each square, to form four ordinary words.

KAHIK

RYPAH

SAQUEY

LUMUTT

WHAT A BELLY
LAUGH IS.

Now arrange the circled letters to form
the surprise answer, as suggested by the
above cartoon.

Print
answer
here

A "◯◯◯◯◯" ◯◯◯◯◯

JUMBLE®

Unscramble these four Jumbles, one letter to each square, to form four ordinary words.

LITAP
☐☐◯◯☐

TUSIE
◯☐◯☐◯

JITNEC
☐☐☐◯◯◯

SPRAYT
◯☐◯☐◯☐

After all I went through to—

THE MOST BRUTAL ASPECT OF BOXING THESE DAYS.

Now arrange the circled letters to form the surprise answer, as suggested by the above cartoon.

Print answer here

THE ◯◯◯◯◯ OF ◯◯◯◯◯

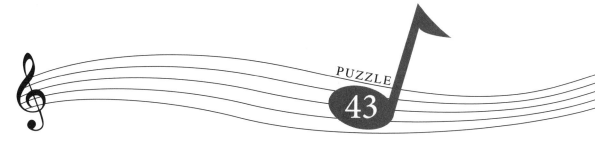

JUMBLE®

Unscramble these four Jumbles, one letter to each square, to form four ordinary words.

GEDUN

USSEO

THERAH

GOHBUT

HOW YOU HAVE TO PAY FOR SOME KINDS OF PLASTIC SURGERY.

Now arrange the circled letters to form the surprise answer, as suggested by the above cartoon.

Print answer here

☐☐☐☐☐☐☐ THE ☐☐☐☐

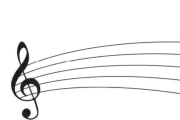

JUMBLE®

Unscramble these four Jumbles, one letter to each square, to form four ordinary words.

IXTYS

VONEY

CAINAM

KALLIA

A MAN WHO TAKES YOU INTO HIS "CONFIDENCE" OFTEN DOES THIS AFTERWARDS.

Now arrange the circled letters to form the surprise answer, as suggested by the above cartoon.

Print answer here JUST ⬚⬚⬚⬚⬚ YOU ⬚⬚

JUMBLE®

Unscramble these four Jumbles, one letter to
each square, to form four ordinary words.

SLARN

CRAFS

REECCO

SNUFUG

Well, I wouldn't say yes
and I wouldn't say no

POLITICAL CANDIDATES
OFTEN STAY ON THE
FENCE IN ORDER TO
AVOID GIVING THIS.

Now arrange the circled letters to form
the surprise answer, as suggested by the
above cartoon.

Print answer here " ⬡⬡ – ⬡⬡⬡⬡⬡ "

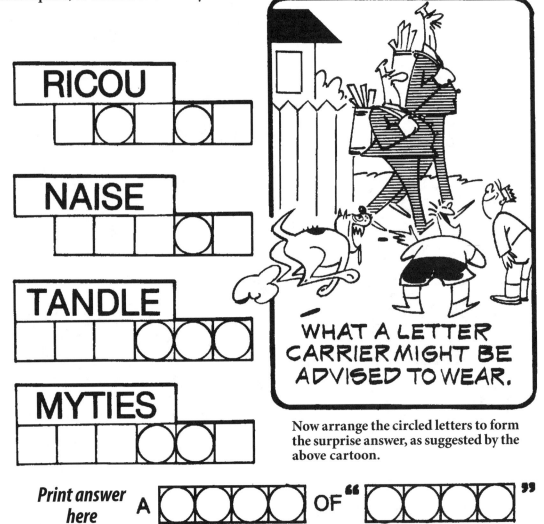

Unscramble these four Jumbles, one letter to each square, to form four ordinary words.

RICOU

NAISE

TANDLE

MYTIES

WHAT A LETTER CARRIER MIGHT BE ADVISED TO WEAR.

Now arrange the circled letters to form the surprise answer, as suggested by the above cartoon.

Print answer here

A ⬡⬡⬡⬡⬡ OF " ⬡⬡⬡⬡⬡ "

48

JUMBLE®

Unscramble these four Jumbles, one letter to
each square, to form four ordinary words.

REVVE

APITO

KESNIC

SWACHE

SOME COLLEGE KIDS
WHO SPEND TOO
MUCH TIME WITH A
PIGSKIN SOMETIMES
FAIL TO GET THIS.

Now arrange the circled letters to form
the surprise answer, as suggested by the
above cartoon.

Print answer here A

JUMBLE®

Unscramble these four Jumbles, one letter to each square, to form four ordinary words.

BATOB

PYXOR

FLUNIX

MADAKS

He wouldn't hurt a flea

WHAT A CHIP ON THE SHOULDER USUALLY IS.

Now arrange the circled letters to form the surprise answer, as suggested by the above cartoon.

Print answer here JUST ☐☐☐☐☐☐ "☐☐☐☐"

JUMBLE®

Unscramble these four Jumbles, one letter to each square, to form four ordinary words.

KANCK

BUCCI

ABANCA

YUIRPT

How much do I owe you from last time?

WHAT MOST OF THE CHIROPRACTOR'S INCOME CAME FROM.

Now arrange the circled letters to form the surprise answer, as suggested by the above cartoon.

Print answer here " ◯◯◯◯ " ◯◯◯

JUMBLE®

Unscramble these four Jumbles, one letter to
each square, to form four ordinary words.

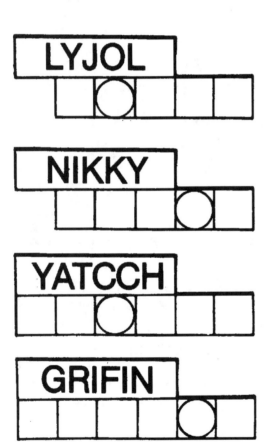

LYJOL

NIKKY

YATCCH

GRIFIN

He'll be sorry

A BACHELOR PREFERS
TO REMAIN
SINGLE, WHILE
OTHERS WOULD THIS.

Now arrange the circled letters to form
the surprise answer, as suggested by the
above cartoon.

Print answer here " ⬡⬡⬡⬡ "

JUMBLE®

Unscramble these four Jumbles, one letter to each square, to form four ordinary words.

OMIDI

AWNTY

COBIXE

YERRSH

WHAT SOME PEOPLE GIVE WHEN THEY LOSE THEIR INHIBITIONS.

Now arrange the circled letters to form the surprise answer, as suggested by the above cartoon.

Print answer here

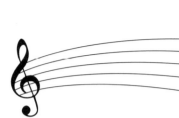

Unscramble these four Jumbles, one letter to
each square, to form four ordinary words.

YOPPP

TREHB

YELARR

IMMORE

HOW HE
ARRANGED THE
SALMON EGGS.

Now arrange the circled letters to form
the surprise answer, as suggested by the
above cartoon.

Print answer here " ⬡⬡⬡ " ⬡⬡ " ⬡⬡⬡ "

JUMBLE®

Unscramble these four Jumbles, one letter to
each square, to form four ordinary words.

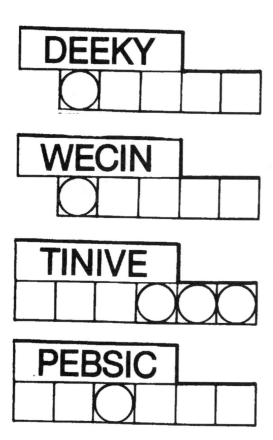

DEEKY

WECIN

TINIVE

PEBSIC

WHAT KIND OF A
GAME IS CROQUET?

Now arrange the circled letters to form
the surprise answer, as suggested by the
above cartoon.

Print answer here   A "⬡⬡⬡⬡⬡⬡" ONE

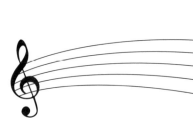

JUMBLE®

Unscramble these four Jumbles, one letter to each square, to form four ordinary words.

YURMK

BROAN

THROXE

URIADS

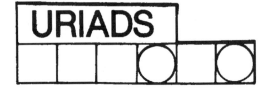

WHAT A BRIDGE PLAYER HAS TO LEARN HOW TO DO.

Now arrange the circled letters to form the surprise answer, as suggested by the above cartoon.

Print answer here

IT ON THE

JUMBLE®

Unscramble these four Jumbles, one letter to each square, to form four ordinary words.

VYNER

RALUR

DIMPOU

NABYRD

WHAT THE COUNTERFEITER WANTED.

Now arrange the circled letters to form the surprise answer, as suggested by the above cartoon.

Print answer here ⬡⬡⬡⬡⬡ " ⬡⬡⬡ "

PUZZLE

56

JUMBLE.

Unscramble these four Jumbles, one letter to
each square, to form four ordinary words.

NEATE

OSOGE

NIMERV

YIELDE

Wish he'd shut up

WHAT SOME PEOPLE
DO WHEN THEY HOLD
A CONVERSATION.

Now arrange the circled letters to form
the surprise answer, as suggested by the
above cartoon.

Print answer here ⬡⬡⬡⬡⬡ ⬡⬡⬡ ⬡⬡

JUMBLE®

Unscramble these four Jumbles, one letter to
each square, to form four ordinary words.

CLOAV

UPYTT

LENETS

DENORM

A SMALL BOY
MIGHT WEAR OUT
EVERYTHING,
INCLUDING THIS.

Now arrange the circled letters to form
the surprise answer, as suggested by the
above cartoon.

Print answer here HIS ◯◯◯◯◯◯◯

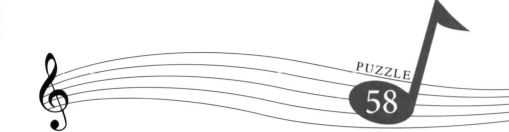

Unscramble these four Jumbles, one letter to each square, to form four ordinary words.

ATLAN

DOUOT

ENGOIP

CHUTOY

They must all be crazy

WHAT FORM OF LOCOMOTION IS DRAG RACING?

Now arrange the circled letters to form the surprise answer, as suggested by the above cartoon.

Print answer here A " ⬡⬡⬡⬡ " ⬡⬡⬡⬡⬡⬡⬡

JUMBLE®

Unscramble these four Jumbles, one letter to each square, to form four ordinary words.

YUMMG

LYRUS

HATHEL

ENVORG

You shoulda seen it

THE "ONE THAT GOT AWAY" WOULD HAVE BEEN BIGGER IF THE FISHERMAN HAD THIS.

Now arrange the circled letters to form the surprise answer, as suggested by the above cartoon.

Print answer here

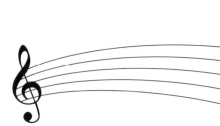

Unscramble these four Jumbles, one letter to each square, to form four ordinary words.

AVARL

ROIVS

PROTTE

UNMOLC

SOME MEN CAN'T BE TRUSTED TOO FAR—OR THIS.

Now arrange the circled letters to form the surprise answer, as suggested by the above cartoon.

Print answer here

JUMBLE®

Unscramble these four Jumbles, one letter to each square, to form four ordinary words.

INYPP
◯◯◯◯◯

CROWE
◯◯◯◯◯

RETAUN
☐☐◯◯◯☐◯

ROYLOP
◯◯◯◯☐◯

Those big shots are always making a killing

A CALCULATOR IS A DEVICE USED BY THESE.

Now arrange the circled letters to form the surprise answer, as suggested by the above cartoon.

Print answer here ◯◯◯◯◯◯ WHO ◯◯◯◯◯

JUMBLE®

Unscramble these four Jumbles, one letter to each square, to form four ordinary words.

WARLC

DYNAH

UNJELG

RINOAT

It's going to take a lot of time

HEALTH CLUB

You can put up with the inconvenience

WHERE YOU MIGHT GO IN ORDER TO MAKE YOURSELF MORE ATTRACTIVE.

Now arrange the circled letters to form the surprise answer, as suggested by the above cartoon.

Print answer here ☐☐☐☐ OF YOUR "☐☐☐☐☐☐"

JUMBLE®

Unscramble these four Jumbles, one letter to each square, to form four ordinary words.

LEWJE

CRANF

THROBE

DEFUAL

YAK YAK

IF YOU'RE NOT CAREFUL ABOUT LENDING AN EAR YOU MIGHT GET THIS.

Now arrange the circled letters to form the surprise answer, as suggested by the above cartoon.

Print answer here IT ⬡⬡⬡⬡⬡⬡ ⬡⬡⬡

JUMBLE®

Unscramble these four Jumbles, one letter to
each square, to form four ordinary words.

KILSY

SAVIT

LACCIO

INLATE

A "STILL" IS
AN APPARATUS
THAT MAKES MANY
PEOPLE THIS.

Now arrange the circled letters to form
the surprise answer, as suggested by the
above cartoon.

Print answer here "  "

66

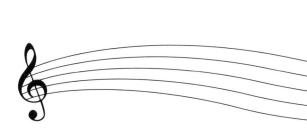

Unscramble these four Jumbles, one letter to
each square, to form four ordinary words.

NAVER

OCHAM

TEFNIC

SOPPEO

CAN YOU TELL ME
WHAT NAPOLEON'S
ORIGIN WAS?

Now arrange the circled letters to form
the surprise answer, as suggested by the
above cartoon.

Print answer here " ◯◯ ◯◯◯◯ - ◯ - ◯◯◯ "

67

JUMBLE®

Unscramble these four Jumbles, one letter to each square, to form four ordinary words.

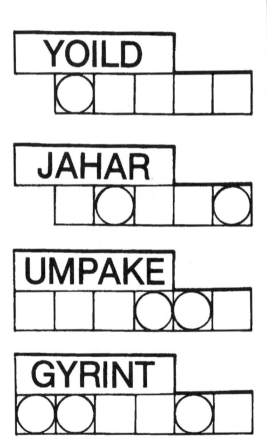

YOILD

JAHAR

UMPAKE

GYRINT

WHAT PEROXIDE MIGHT DO.

Now arrange the circled letters to form the surprise answer, as suggested by the above cartoon.

Print answer here ⬡⬡⬡⬡ HER ⬡⬡⬡⬡

JUMBLE®

Unscramble these four Jumbles, one letter to
each square, to form four ordinary words.

PRAAT

SHEWO

NUGMIP

PRAMTE

SOME PEOPLE
WITH THE GIFT OF
GAB NEVER KNOW
WHEN TO DO THIS.

Now arrange the circled letters to form
the surprise answer, as suggested by the
above cartoon.

Print answer here

JUMBLE®

Unscramble these four Jumbles, one letter to each square, to form four ordinary words.

BUAQS

WETIC

INMAYL

BIFCAR

THAT SNOBBISH SKUNK WAS UNPOPULAR BECAUSE HE WAS ALWAYS PUTTING ON THIS.

Now arrange the circled letters to form the surprise answer, as suggested by the above cartoon.

Print answer here SUCH ⃝⃝⃝⃝⃝ " ⃝⃝⃝⃝ "

JUMBLE®

Unscramble these four Jumbles, one letter to each square, to form four ordinary words.

PEBID

BUMIE

EXTUDO

GAMNEA

Forget it

$75,000

WHAT TO
DO WHEN YOU
HAVE THE FEELING
YOU WANT TO
SPEND MORE THAN
YOU CAN AFFORD.

Now arrange the circled letters to form the surprise answer, as suggested by the above cartoon.

Print answer here

◯◯◯◯ IT IN THE " ◯◯◯ – ◯◯◯ "

JUMBLE®

Unscramble these four Jumbles, one letter to each square, to form four ordinary words.

HOOPT

DAFEM

DECAFE

LAWHOL

Now, now—listen to reason

THE BEST THING TO HAVE IN A HEATED DISCUSSION.

Now arrange the circled letters to form the surprise answer, as suggested by the above cartoon.

Print answer here A ⬡⬡⬡⬡ ⬡⬡⬡⬡

72

JUMBLE®

Unscramble these four Jumbles, one letter to each square, to form four ordinary words.

TYTUN

HELEW

LEEMOT

NOBBOA

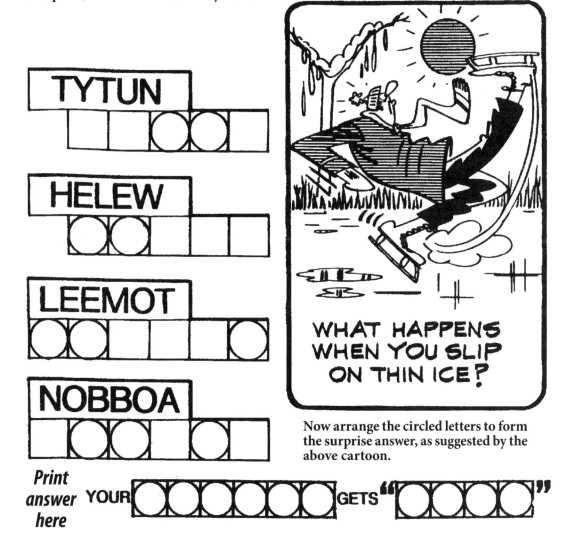

WHAT HAPPENS WHEN YOU SLIP ON THIN ICE?

Now arrange the circled letters to form the surprise answer, as suggested by the above cartoon.

Print answer here YOUR ⬡⬡⬡⬡⬡ GETS "⬡⬡⬡⬡"

JUMBLE®

Unscramble these four Jumbles, one letter to each square, to form four ordinary words.

YIKTT

GOLIC

BOBJER

SCUABA

WHAT TWO WRONGS SOMETIMES ACTUALLY DO MAKE.

Now arrange the circled letters to form the surprise answer, as suggested by the above cartoon.

Print answer here ☐ " ☐☐☐☐ "

JUMBLE®

Unscramble these four Jumbles, one letter to each square, to form four ordinary words.

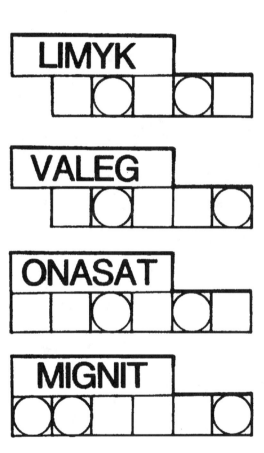

LIMYK

VALEG

ONASAT

MIGNIT

HE HAD THE SELF-CONTROL TO GIVE UP DRINKING AND SMOKING BUT NOT THE SELF-CONTROL TO GIVE UP THIS.

Now arrange the circled letters to form the surprise answer, as suggested by the above cartoon.

Print answer here  ABOUT

JUMBLE®

Unscramble these four Jumbles, one letter to each square, to form four ordinary words.

SUMIN

COSUR

GOYAVE

RUPPLE

They won the lottery!

So what?

IF IT SOUNDS LIKE A "WHINE," IT'S PROBABLY A COMPLAINT THAT COMES FROM THIS.

Now arrange the circled letters to form the surprise answer, as suggested by the above cartoon.

Print answer here ◯◯◯◯ ◯◯◯◯◯◯◯

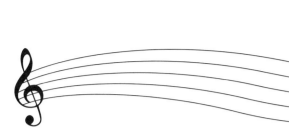

Unscramble these four Jumbles, one letter to each square, to form four ordinary words.

OUDES

TOIDI

SABBOR

KLEESH

WHAT A SELF-
EMPLOYED PERSON IS
NEVER APT TO DO.

Now arrange the circled letters to form the surprise answer, as suggested by the above cartoon.

Print answer here ⬚⬚⬚⬚⬚⬚⬚ THE ⬚⬚⬚⬚

JUMBLE®

Unscramble these four Jumbles, one letter to each square, to form four ordinary words.

WONNK

ZAHLE

TEYQUI

CRAGOU

Why not also take my house and car?

THAT NEXT-DOOR NEIGHBOR WHO'S ALWAYS BORROWING YOUR STUFF WILL TAKE ANYTHING FROM YOU EXCEPT THIS.

Now arrange the circled letters to form the surprise answer, as suggested by the above cartoon.

Print answer here ⬚ ⬚⬚⬚⬚

JUMBLE®

Unscramble these four Jumbles, one letter to
each square, to form four ordinary words.

GUGOE

ULIQT

DOYLEM

HESTEE

WHAT A MEAN
MAN WHO WOULD
STEAL CANDY
FROM A BABY IS.

Now arrange the circled letters to form
the surprise answer, as suggested by the
above cartoon.

Print answer
here   A ⬜⬜⬜⬜ WITHOUT " ⬜⬜⬜⬜ "
        A

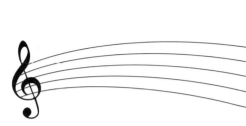

Unscramble these four Jumbles, one letter to
each square, to form four ordinary words.

GINTY

CNOTH

MUSSIE

SAVILE

WHAT THE BOY
SNAKE SAID TO
THE GIRL SNAKE.

Now arrange the circled letters to form
the surprise answer, as suggested by the
above cartoon.

Print answer here ◯◯◯◯ US A ◯◯◯◯

JUMBLE®

Unscramble these four Jumbles, one letter to each square, to form four ordinary words.

DEACK

LEREB

RENARB

ONSWID

Lovely day

Yeah, but for tomorrow rain is forecast

A PESSIMIST IS ALWAYS GOOD FOR THIS.

Now arrange the circled letters to form the surprise answer, as suggested by the above cartoon.

Print answer here

81

JUMBLE®

Unscramble these four Jumbles, one letter to each square, to form four ordinary words.

DKVOA

MTEEH

LWIWOL

CTEOKP

WHEN LITTLE RAYMOND ROMANO WAS BORN ON 12-21-57, EVERYBODY ----

Now arrange the circled letters to form the surprise answer, as suggested by the above cartoon.

Print answer here

82

JUMBLE.

Unscramble these four Jumbles, one letter to each square, to form four ordinary words.

SOJIT

FDYFA

SLTUCP

PPEMIL

THE QUARTERBACK DID THIS AFTER BEING PRESENTED WITH THE ENDORSEMENT DEAL.

Now arrange the circled letters to form the surprise answer, as suggested by the above cartoon.

Print answer here

JUMBLE®

Unscramble these four Jumbles, one letter to each square, to form four ordinary words.

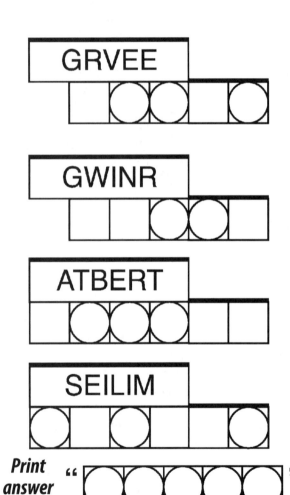

GRVEE

GWINR

ATBERT

SEILIM

VALLEY AVE. IN
BANGOR IS A ---

Now arrange the circled letters to form the surprise answer, as suggested by the above cartoon.

Print answer here " ◯◯◯◯◯ " ◯◯◯◯◯◯

JUMBLE®

Unscramble these four Jumbles, one letter to
each square, to form four ordinary words.

GREUP

DPEUN

CARODC

SIGNEU

I'm so glad everyone is here. It's so great to see everyone.

SHE LIKED SEEING ALL THE
PRESENTS, BUT SHE REALLY
LIKED EVERYONE'S ---

Now arrange the circled letters to form
the surprise answer, as suggested by the
above cartoon.

Print answer here

JUMBLE®

Unscramble these four Jumbles, one letter to each square, to form four ordinary words.

YORRS

EECFN

YALVEL

OITTUF

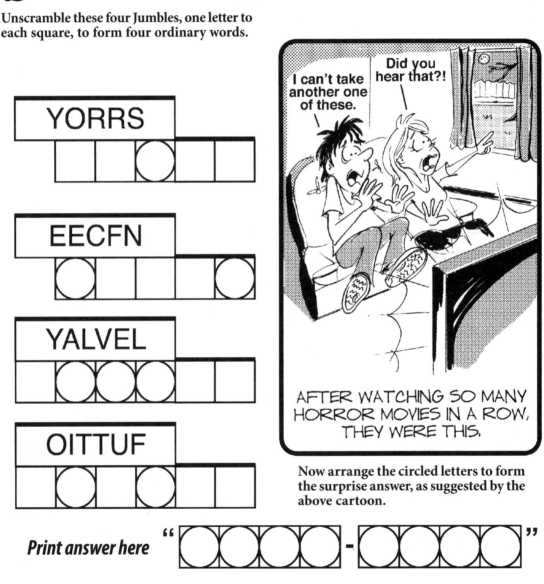

I can't take another one of these.

Did you hear that?!

AFTER WATCHING SO MANY HORROR MOVIES IN A ROW, THEY WERE THIS.

Now arrange the circled letters to form the surprise answer, as suggested by the above cartoon.

Print answer here " ◯◯◯◯◯ - ◯◯◯◯ "

JUMBLE®

Unscramble these four Jumbles, one letter to
each square, to form four ordinary words.

CMHUN

DOITI

DDEEGH

WINNUD

Well, we got it
wrong, but I
think he'll be
fine.

DR. FRANKENSTEIN PUT
A FAULTY BRAIN IN HIS
MONSTER, BUT THE
MONSTER ----

Now arrange the circled letters to form
the surprise answer, as suggested by the
above cartoon.

Print answer here

'

JUMBLE®

Unscramble these four Jumbles, one letter to each square, to form four ordinary words.

COKBL

NCRAH

RANLEY

DIOWSM

Congrats, Judge!

Let's start on the next 100.

PRESIDING OVER 100 TRIALS WAS THIS FOR THE JUDGE.

Now arrange the circled letters to form the surprise answer, as suggested by the above cartoon.

Print answer here A ◯◯◯◯◯◯◯◯◯

JUMBLE®

Unscramble these four Jumbles, one letter to each square, to form four ordinary words.

SLIOP

KEWAA

NATDEN

YCUDOL

How is everything?

This is perfect!

AFTER TASTING HIS PERFECTLY COOKED, MEDIUM-RARE STEAK, THE CUSTOMER SAID THIS.

Now arrange the circled letters to form the surprise answer, as suggested by the above cartoon.

Print answer here

JUMBLE®

Unscramble these four Jumbles, one letter to each square, to form four ordinary words.

NOLEV

TCETO

SLEONS

DAPRAE

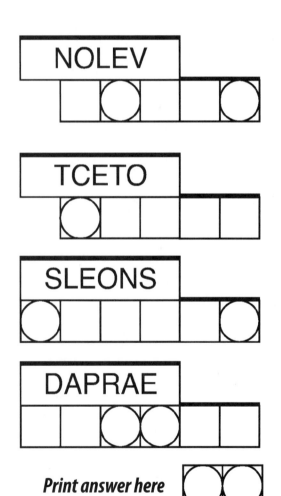

Business is so good that I'm going to have to open another location.

I can't decide: white, wheat, sourdough...

Named Best Sandwich 5th Year in a row!

AS THE OWNER OF THE MOST SUCCESSFUL SANDWICH SHOP IN TOWN, HE WAS THIS.

Now arrange the circled letters to form the surprise answer, as suggested by the above cartoon.

Print answer here ◯◯ ◯ ◯◯◯◯◯

JUMBLE®

Unscramble these four Jumbles, one letter to each square, to form four ordinary words.

GITTH

SLSIB

KANBIG

MRUEES

I don't recognize this place. Let's try going that way.

I thought we were headed this way.

SMOKEY GOT LOST IN THE WOODS AFTER HE LOST THIS.

Now arrange the circled letters to form the surprise answer, as suggested by the above cartoon.

Print answer here

JUMBLE®

Unscramble these four Jumbles, one letter to
each square, to form four ordinary words.

LIPTO

OZAKO

HURNKS

TALLEY

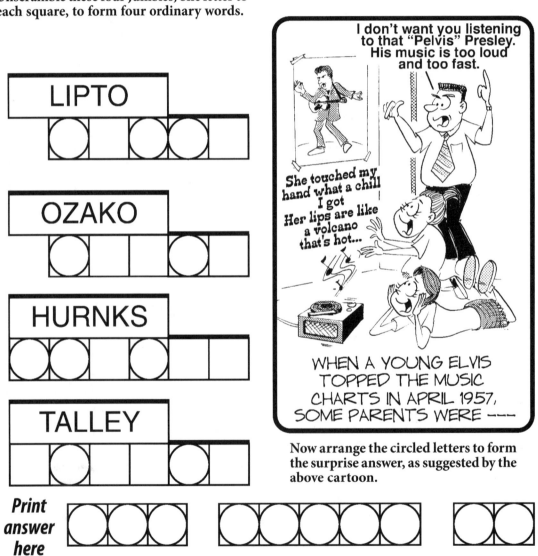

I don't want you listening
to that "Pelvis" Presley.
His music is too loud
and too fast.

She touched my
hand what a chill
I got
Her lips are like
a volcano
that's hot...

WHEN A YOUNG ELVIS
TOPPED THE MUSIC
CHARTS IN APRIL 1957,
SOME PARENTS WERE ---

Now arrange the circled letters to form
the surprise answer, as suggested by the
above cartoon.

*Print
answer
here*

JUMBLE®

Unscramble these four Jumbles, one letter to each square, to form four ordinary words.

GETRI

LNUGC

RUNBEM

NIEGUS

Racers Welcome!

I'll need you to restock the new shoes and shorts.

Sure thing, Boss.

THE MARATHON WINNER'S FAVORITE PART OF OWNING HIS OWN STORE WAS ---

Now arrange the circled letters to form the surprise answer, as suggested by the above cartoon.

Print answer here

JUMBLE®

Unscramble these four Jumbles, one letter to each square, to form four ordinary words.

ROLOF

TALOG

CANGLE

SOIPEM

Are you all cleaned up and ready to take the plunge?

Ouch! I just nicked myself.

BEFORE THE WEDDING CEREMONY, THE HUSBAND-TO-BE WAS ---

Now arrange the circled letters to form the surprise answer, as suggested by the above cartoon.

Print answer here

94

JUMBLE

Unscramble these four Jumbles, one letter to
each square, to form four ordinary words.

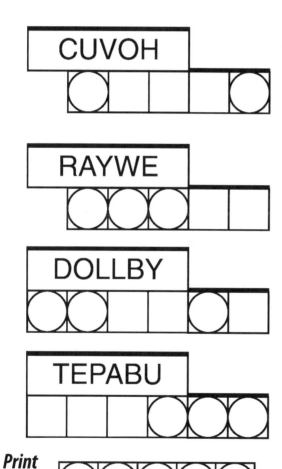

CUVOH

RAYWE

DOLLBY

TEPABU

Stop him.
He's getting
away!

Freeze!
Come
back
here!

THE BIRD DECIDED TO
STEAL THE DIAMOND
NECKLACE BECAUSE HE
FELT HE WAS ---

Now arrange the circled letters to form
the surprise answer, as suggested by the
above cartoon.

*Print
answer
here*

JUMBLE®

Unscramble these four Jumbles, one letter to each square, to form four ordinary words.

UDEEL

REMHY

FENTIC

PLURBA

Is this an African or Asian species?

It doesn't matter. He's going to be a HUGE draw.

ZOO LOADING ZONE

WHETHER OR NOT THE ZOO'S NEW PACHYDERM WAS FROM AFRICA OR ASIA WAS ----

Now arrange the circled letters to form the surprise answer, as suggested by the above cartoon.

Print answer here " "

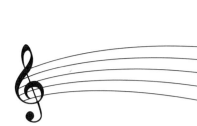

JUMBLE®

Unscramble these four Jumbles, one letter to
each square, to form four ordinary words.

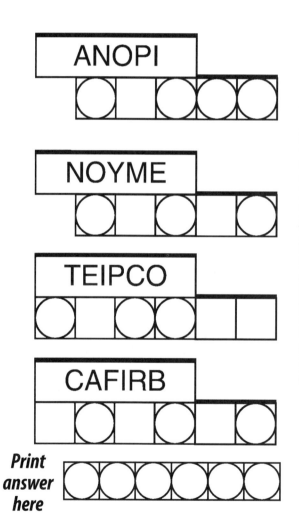

ANOPI

NOYME

TEIPCO

CAFIRB

Print answer here

THE BUSINESS OWNED BY
THE MOM AND DAD
WAS A ---

Now arrange the circled letters to form
the surprise answer, as suggested by the
above cartoon.

PUZZLE
95

Honey, we just added another business.

Dad, we're out of cereal.

Mommy will be right with you after she finishes this deal.

Mommy, where's bunny?

97

JUMBLE®

Unscramble these four Jumbles, one letter to each square, to form four ordinary words.

VINEG

CHUNB

RUYNIJ

SAJDUT

This was a really smart move.

It will pay for itself in no time.

It's certainly sunny enough.

THEY INSTALLED SOLAR PANELS ON THEIR HOUSE BECAUSE IT WAS A ---

Now arrange the circled letters to form the surprise answer, as suggested by the above cartoon.

Print answer here

JUMBLE®

Unscramble these four Jumbles, one letter to each square, to form four ordinary words.

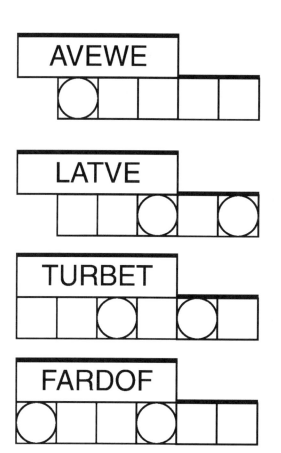

AVEWE

LATVE

TURBET

FARDOF

I'm sorry. The gate is closed.

I told you we should have valet parked.

You took the long way!

C-29

THE TWINS MISSED THEIR FLIGHT BECAUSE THEY WERE ---

Now arrange the circled letters to form the surprise answer, as suggested by the above cartoon.

Print answer here  " ◯◯◯ " ◯◯◯◯◯

JUMBLE®

Unscramble these four Jumbles, one letter to each square, to form four ordinary words.

AGGUE

SEMYS

SAHNIV

THIRME

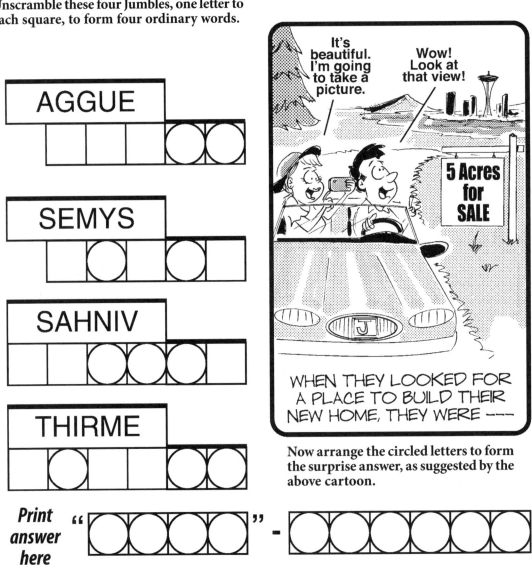

WHEN THEY LOOKED FOR A PLACE TO BUILD THEIR NEW HOME, THEY WERE ----

Now arrange the circled letters to form the surprise answer, as suggested by the above cartoon.

Print answer here " ☐☐☐☐ " - ☐☐☐☐☐☐

JUMBLE®

Unscramble these four Jumbles, one letter to each square, to form four ordinary words.

MCPIR

KAROC

CHETAD

ROTECK

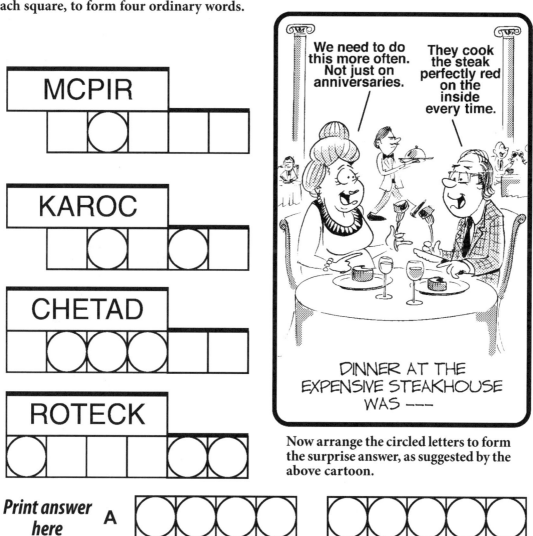

We need to do this more often. Not just on anniversaries.

They cook the steak perfectly red on the inside every time.

DINNER AT THE EXPENSIVE STEAKHOUSE WAS ---

Now arrange the circled letters to form the surprise answer, as suggested by the above cartoon.

Print answer here A

101

JUMBLE®

Unscramble these four Jumbles, one letter to each square, to form four ordinary words.

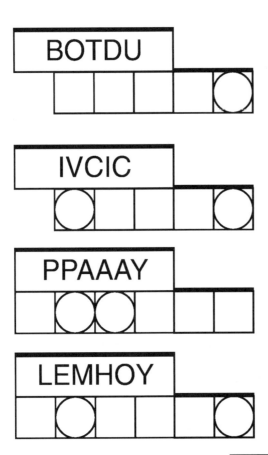

BOTDU

IVCIC

PPAAAY

LEMHOY

THE TIGER'S TWIN BROTHER WAS A ---

Now arrange the circled letters to form the surprise answer, as suggested by the above cartoon.

Print answer here

102

JUMBLE®

Unscramble these four Jumbles, one letter to
each square, to form four ordinary words.

HETFI

GAMIE

RESHOK

INIOCC

I've been saving up for this. I hope you like it.

Like it? I love it! It has every-thing- cooler, remote, cup holder, foot massage, everything.

WHEN SHE BOUGHT HER HUSBAND A FANCY NEW RECLINER, HE PROMISED TO ---

Now arrange the circled letters to form
the surprise answer, as suggested by the
above cartoon.

Print answer here " ◯◯◯◯◯ - ◯◯◯ " ◯◯

JUMBLE®

Unscramble these four Jumbles, one letter to each square, to form four ordinary words.

CAMWA

MERFA

VNEEEL

TIEYUQ

I love having more grand-babies.

His branch is all ready for him

He looks just like his father.

THE BABY MONKEY WAS BORN IN THE ----

Now arrange the circled letters to form the surprise answer, as suggested by the above cartoon.

Print answer here

JUMBLE®

Unscramble these four Jumbles, one letter to
each square, to form four ordinary words.

MEEEC

LFYUL

BRABEJ

RAMBEK

Well, when
you have
a superior
swing like
me, trees cut
like butter.
I can give you
some pointers.

Someone
needs to cut
him down to
size.

I'll give
YOU a
pointer.

THEY DIDN'T LIKE WORKING
WITH THE OBNOXIOUS TREE
CUTTER BECAUSE HE
WAS A ----

Now arrange the circled letters to form
the surprise answer, as suggested by the
above cartoon.

Print answer "◯◯◯◯◯◯◯◯◯◯"
here

105

JUMBLE®

Unscramble these four Jumbles, one letter to each square, to form four ordinary words.

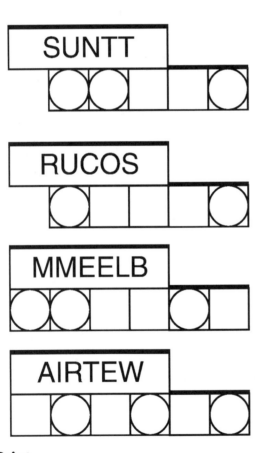

SUNTT

RUCOS

MMEELB

AIRTEW

THEY RENTED AN
APARTMENT ON THAT
PARTICULAR ROAD
BECAUSE THEY WERE ----

Now arrange the circled letters to form the surprise answer, as suggested by the above cartoon.

Print
answer
here

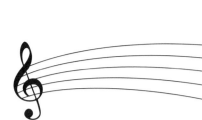

Unscramble these four Jumbles, one letter to each square, to form four ordinary words.

LASSH

PURET

TAREOT

CUPENO

THEY WENT SNORKELING TO ---

Now arrange the circled letters to form the surprise answer, as suggested by the above cartoon.

Print answer here " ⬡⬡⬡ " ⬡⬡⬡⬡⬡⬡⬡

JUMBLE®

Unscramble these four Jumbles, one letter to
each square, to form four ordinary words.

INGAA

GEMAO

DONSWI

METBON

Oh, my! Woody
destroyed
my flowers.

He tunneled
out again.
I'll go look for
him.

WHEN HE REALIZED THAT
THEIR GOLDEN RETRIEVER
WASN'T IN THE BACKYARD,
HE SAID ---

Now arrange the circled letters to form
the surprise answer, as suggested by the
above cartoon.

Print answer
here   " ◯◯◯ - ◯◯◯◯ - ◯◯ "

JUMBLE®

Unscramble these four Jumbles, one letter to each square, to form four ordinary words.

NARPK

DIVOA

TULIDE

NEEGAG

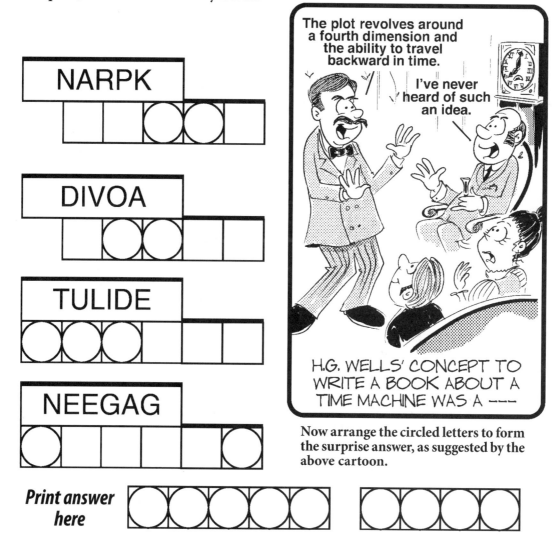

The plot revolves around a fourth dimension and the ability to travel backward in time.

I've never heard of such an idea.

H.G. WELLS' CONCEPT TO WRITE A BOOK ABOUT A TIME MACHINE WAS A ----

Now arrange the circled letters to form the surprise answer, as suggested by the above cartoon.

Print answer here

JUMBLE®

Unscramble these four Jumbles, one letter to each square, to form four ordinary words.

ROLGY

DNIRK

PNILST

TENZIH

They always swing at my split-finger fastball.

That's the way I get them to swing too.

THE RESEMBLANCE BETWEEN THE PITCHERS WAS ----

Now arrange the circled letters to form the surprise answer, as suggested by the above cartoon.

Print answer here

JUMBLE®

Unscramble these four Jumbles, one letter to
each square, to form four ordinary words.

NURGT

AREPO

SNUTUJ

LUGFEN

What do
you say?
Would you
like a mink
coat?

Are you
kidding
me?

OFF-SEASON DISCOUNTS

BIG
MINK
SALE

WHEN HE ASKED HER IF SHE
WANTED A NEW MINK COAT,
SHE SAID ---

Now arrange the circled letters to form
the surprise answer, as suggested by the
above cartoon.

Print answer here " ◯◯◯ " ◯◯◯◯

JUMBLE®

Unscramble these four Jumbles, one letter to each square, to form four ordinary words.

DINYW

FIRDT

PESYEL

LIBAVE

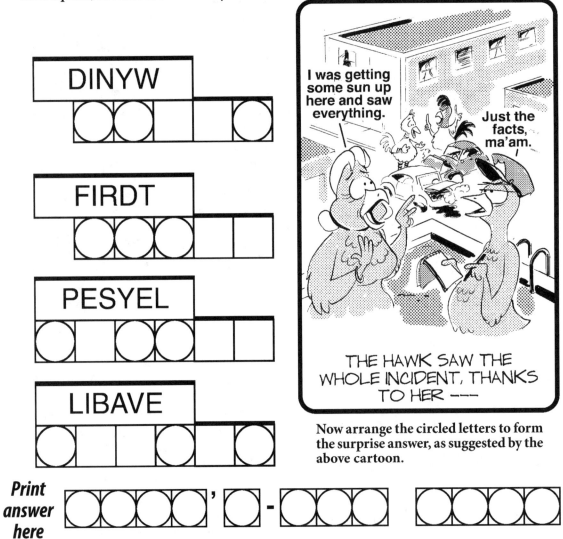

I was getting some sun up here and saw everything.

Just the facts, ma'am.

THE HAWK SAW THE WHOLE INCIDENT, THANKS TO HER ---

Now arrange the circled letters to form the surprise answer, as suggested by the above cartoon.

Print answer here

112

JUMBLE®

Unscramble these four Jumbles, one letter to each square, to form four ordinary words.

ROPIR

SEGUT

TOXCIE

TAMETR

Honey, do you know where the Jumble is?

Yes. It's there, there and there.

THE PUPPY THAT SHREDDED THE MORNING NEWSPAPER WAS A ---

Now arrange the circled letters to form the surprise answer, as suggested by the above cartoon.

Print answer here " ⟨◯◯◯◯⟩ - ⟨◯◯◯⟩ "

113

JUMBLE®

Unscramble these four Jumbles, one letter to each square, to form four ordinary words.

SEGUS

RIBBE

RECYLE

CUPANK

You have contracts for hunting vests and hats to sign.

Wow! This is going to be a good season.

THE STAR OF THE NEW "DEER HUNTER" SHOW WAS BEGINNING TO ----

Now arrange the circled letters to form the surprise answer, as suggested by the above cartoon.

Print answer here

JUMBLE®

Unscramble these four Jumbles, one letter to each square, to form four ordinary words.

LORDL

DIBEA

OLOGAN

HOTAFM

THE FLEET OF GIANT OCTOPUSES WAS AN ---

Now arrange the circled letters to form the surprise answer, as suggested by the above cartoon.

Print answer here

JUMBLE®

Unscramble these four Jumbles, one letter to
each square, to form four ordinary words.

VREIR

NASTD

OLEVIT

NERLTE

Hello, Ben!
Love the
spectacles!

These have
changed
my life.

I knew
they
would.

BIFOCALS WERE BECOMING
AS POPULAR AS
BEN FRANKLIN ----

Now arrange the circled letters to form
the surprise answer, as suggested by the
above cartoon.

**Print answer
here**

JUMBLE®

Unscramble these four Jumbles, one letter to each square, to form four ordinary words.

SYOBS

TINYU

DONTER

NURREN

This downpour is so heavy!

I'm scared.

CAMPING DURING THE THUNDERSTORM WAS ---

Now arrange the circled letters to form the surprise answer, as suggested by the above cartoon.

Print answer here "◯◯ - ◯◯◯◯◯◯"

JUMBLE®

Unscramble these four Jumbles, one letter to each square, to form four ordinary words.

FURGF

FINKE

ALITUR

ABOPIH

Great look, dude!

Well, thank you. Thank you very much.

ELVIS PRESLEY'S NEW CUSTOM-MADE SUIT WAS ---

Now arrange the circled letters to form the surprise answer, as suggested by the above cartoon.

Print answer here

JUMBLE®

Unscramble these four Jumbles, one letter to each square, to form four ordinary words.

GOBSU

LNITG

SICOAF

ARAYIV

So, is it going to rain today?

I believe it will be partly sunny and 77 degrees the rest of the day.

THE WEATHERMAN BOUGHT THE NEW FISHING POLE ----

Now arrange the circled letters to form the surprise answer, as suggested by the above cartoon.

Print answer here

⬭⬭⬭ ⬭⬭⬭⬭⬭⬭⬭

119

JUMBLE®

Unscramble these four Jumbles, one letter to each square, to form four ordinary words.

SAYBS

NLAKP

ONRUCK

ZORNFE

Look, kid, you can be the most artistically perfect performer in the world, but audiences can be brutal! If you're not fired up, it's Endsville.

Wow! Thanks for the advice, Mr. Sinatra, sir.

WHEN SINATRA GAVE THE YOUNG SINGER ADVICE, HE ---

Now arrange the circled letters to form the surprise answer, as suggested by the above cartoon.

Print answer here

JUMBLE®

Unscramble these four Jumbles, one letter to each square, to form four ordinary words.

DAGEL

VOREP

GLITHP

TYNPAR

Hi, honey! I just can't wait until I see you again. I love you so much. Will you marry me?

Yes! Yes, I will.

HE COULDN'T WAIT TO PROPOSE TO HIS GIRLFRIEND IN PERSON, SO HE ---

Now arrange the circled letters to form the surprise answer, as suggested by the above cartoon.

Print answer here

JUMBLE®

Unscramble these four Jumbles, one letter to
each square, to form four ordinary words.

CENEF

CLUEN

HLIRLS

TISISN

THE HELSINKI MARATHON
ENDED AT
THE ---

Now arrange the circled letters to form
the surprise answer, as suggested by the
above cartoon.

Print
answer
here

" ◯◯◯◯◯◯◯ " ◯◯◯◯

JUMBLE®

Unscramble these four Jumbles, one letter to each square, to form four ordinary words.

HIREK

DUMYD

EEGULD

CAPTIM

WHEN IT CAME TO GETTING NEW BUSINESS, THE MUSICAL INSTRUMENT STORE ---

Now arrange the circled letters to form the surprise answer, as suggested by the above cartoon.

Print answer here

123

JUMBLE®

Unscramble these four Jumbles, one letter to each square, to form four ordinary words.

BNALK

ODORE

PADTUE

SPOISG

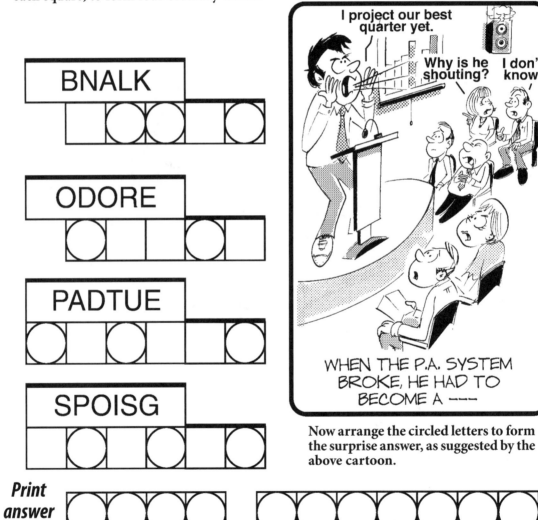

I project our best quarter yet.

Why is he shouting?

I don't know.

WHEN THE P.A. SYSTEM BROKE, HE HAD TO BECOME A ----

Now arrange the circled letters to form the surprise answer, as suggested by the above cartoon.

Print answer here

JUMBLE®

Unscramble these four Jumbles, one letter to each square, to form four ordinary words.

HARCP

MIDTA

NARUTT

REWEPT

Remember, men, a good game plan that you act on today can be better than a perfect one tomorrow.

Uh, yes, sir?

THE ARMY BASE HAD A SOFTBALL TEAM AND THE GENERAL WAS THE – – – –

Now arrange the circled letters to form the surprise answer, as suggested by the above cartoon.

Print answer here

125

JUMBLE®

Unscramble these four Jumbles, one letter to each square, to form four ordinary words.

VEERF

LUVAT

TINDAY

WESTEF

WHEN THE COACH TOOK HIM OUT OF THE GAME, THE STARTING PITCHER WAS ----

Now arrange the circled letters to form the surprise answer, as suggested by the above cartoon.

Print answer here

JUMBLE®

Unscramble these four Jumbles, one letter to
each square, to form four ordinary words.

RABNO

SEYMS

STOPLA

UTARIL

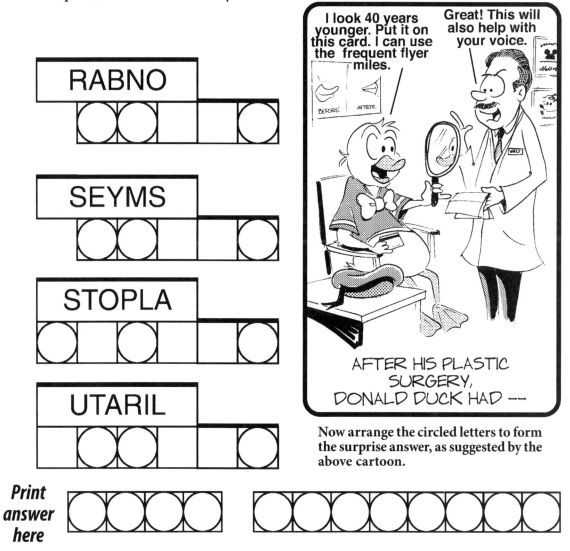

I look 40 years younger. Put it on this card. I can use the frequent flyer miles.

BEFORE   AFTER

Great! This will also help with your voice.

WALT

AFTER HIS PLASTIC SURGERY, DONALD DUCK HAD --

Now arrange the circled letters to form
the surprise answer, as suggested by the
above cartoon.

**Print
answer
here**

JUMBLE®

Unscramble these four Jumbles, one letter to each square, to form four ordinary words.

DUSKO

NIRBG

WARLEY

SIMACO

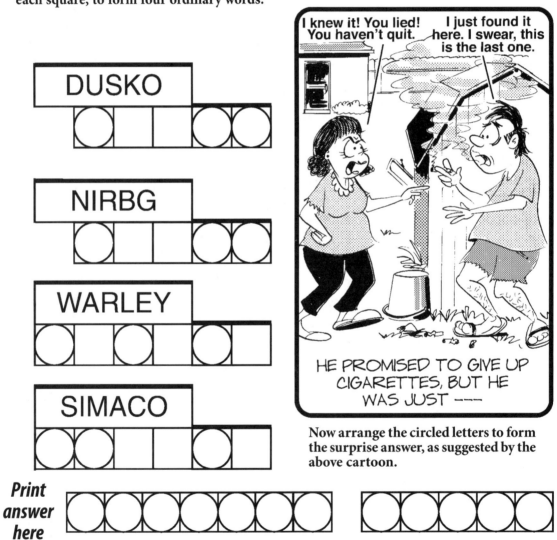

I knew it! You lied! You haven't quit.

I just found it here. I swear, this is the last one.

HE PROMISED TO GIVE UP CIGARETTES, BUT HE WAS JUST ----

Now arrange the circled letters to form the surprise answer, as suggested by the above cartoon.

Print answer here

JUMBLE®

Unscramble these four Jumbles, one letter to each square, to form four ordinary words.

RAYIN

LADVI

TARORO

VTELEV

He's been at it all day.

Practice makes perfect.

HE PRACTICED THE HIGH JUMP ---

Now arrange the circled letters to form the surprise answer, as suggested by the above cartoon.

Print answer here

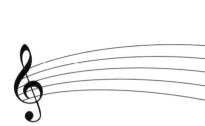

Unscramble these four Jumbles, one letter to each square, to form four ordinary words.

TRECP

SUYMH

TIDFET

CUCUSA

Sorry I'm late.

It's about time.

Well, maybe I won't play on time when he starts.

I can't even look at him.

AFTER ARRIVING LATE, THE SYMPHONY CONDUCTOR ---

Now arrange the circled letters to form the surprise answer, as suggested by the above cartoon.

Print answer here

JUMBLE®

Unscramble these four Jumbles, one letter to
each square, to form four ordinary words.

LNAKF

PUSOY

RIDCAN

WHERSD

Whew! It scares me
every time he slides.

He did it!
He scored!

AFTER THE COLLISION AT
HOME PLATE, THE PLAYER'S
MOTHER WAS GLAD
HE WAS ---

Now arrange the circled letters to form
the surprise answer, as suggested by the
above cartoon.

Print
answer
here

131

JUMBLE

Unscramble these four Jumbles, one letter to
each square, to form four ordinary words.

SLATB

CLERI

WRINYE

GLEFAN

Have a great day!
I'll see you after
work.

I'm going to
run to the
driving range
for some
practice on
the way
home.

I JMBL

HE WANTED TO PRACTICE
WITH HIS NEW CLUBS,
SO HE PLANNED TO ----

Now arrange the circled letters to form
the surprise answer, as suggested by the
above cartoon.

Print
answer
here

JUMBLE®

Unscramble these four Jumbles, one letter to each square, to form four ordinary words.

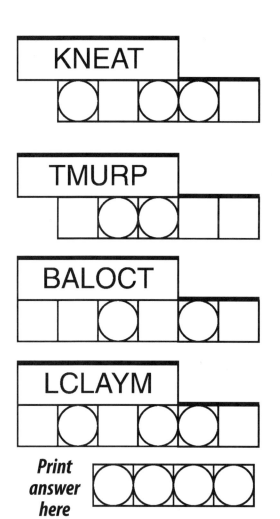

KNEAT

TMURP

BALOCT

LCLAYM

Print answer here

This is a good time to buy.

I need to increase my herd.

THE CATTLE RANCHER WANTED TO STOCK UP, SO HE WENT TO THE ---

Now arrange the circled letters to form the surprise answer, as suggested by the above cartoon.

JUMBLE®

Unscramble these four Jumbles, one letter to each square, to form four ordinary words.

ZIREP

INGAA

BULMET

EEENDL

I told you to give it up. And leave Buffy alone!

It's going to transport her just like on Star Trek.

HE TRIED TO BUILD A WORKING TELEPORTER, BUT HIS PLANS NEVER ----

Now arrange the circled letters to form the surprise answer, as suggested by the above cartoon.

Print answer here

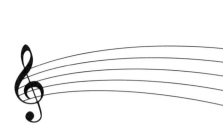

Unscramble these four Jumbles, one letter to each square, to form four ordinary words.

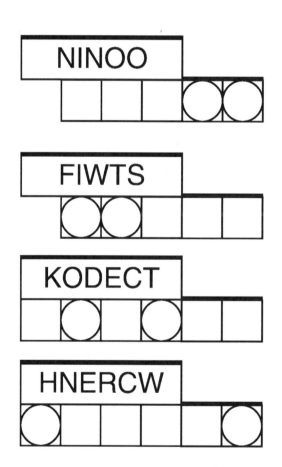

NINOO

FIWTS

KODECT

HNERCW

Do you think you'll get to the top?

I hope.

We'll see.

ASKED IF THEIR BAND WOULD SCORE, PETE TOWNSHEND AND ROGER DALTREY SAID ---

Now arrange the circled letters to form the surprise answer, as suggested by the above cartoon.

Print answer here

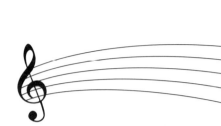

Unscramble these four Jumbles, one letter to each square, to form four ordinary words.

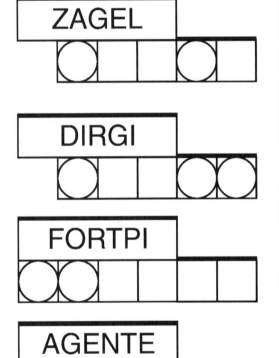

ZAGEL

DIRGI

FORTPI

AGENTE

And the winner of the 50/50 raffle is number 1066.

50/50 $1000.00 Drawing

You won!

Oh, my! This is wonderful!

SHE THOUGHT THAT WINNING THE $1,000 IN THE RAFFLE WAS A ----

Now arrange the circled letters to form the surprise answer, as suggested by the above cartoon.

Print answer here

JUMBLE®

Unscramble these four Jumbles, one letter to each square, to form four ordinary words.

YECDA

LIQTU

NINEEG

CONPUE

AFTER A HECTIC DAY, HE WAS HAPPY TO HAVE THIS TO EAT HIS SLICE OF PIZZA ---

Now arrange the circled letters to form the surprise answer, as suggested by the above cartoon.

Print answer here

" ☐☐☐☐☐ " ☐☐☐ ☐☐☐☐☐

JUMBLE®

Unscramble these four Jumbles, one letter to
each square, to form four ordinary words.

LECOL
◯◯◯◯

YAROL
◯◯◯◯◯

FLUDON
◯◯◯

WONIDW
◯◯◯◯

Look at
them go.

They sure
know how to
have fun.

AFTER THE CIRCUS ENDED,
SOME OF THE PERFORMERS
LIKED TO ---

Now arrange the circled letters to form
the surprise answer, as suggested by the
above cartoon.

Print
answer
here
◯◯◯◯◯   ◯◯◯◯◯◯◯

JUMBLE®

Unscramble these four Jumbles, one letter to each square, to form four ordinary words.

VAINA

GRACO

WIDMIT

SMELUC

Listen! You never go out. You ARE going out with Rick's friend Friday night.

Who died and made you boss?

SHE WANTED HER SISTER TO FIND A GUY TO GO OUT WITH, SO SHE GAVE HER A ---

Now arrange the circled letters to form the surprise answer, as suggested by the above cartoon.

Print answer here

139

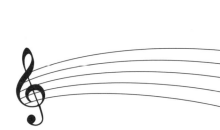

Unscramble these four Jumbles, one letter to each square, to form four ordinary words.

GOLIO

DILUF

SHONEC

VIRLDE

CASPER'S DATE FOR THE HALLOWEEN PARTY WAS HIS ----

Now arrange the circled letters to form the surprise answer, as suggested by the above cartoon.

Print answer here " ◯◯◯◯◯ " - ◯◯◯◯◯◯◯

JUMBLE

Unscramble these four Jumbles, one letter to each square, to form four ordinary words.

UMUSH

TENGA

DEETIC

GORGYG

EVERYONE LOVED THE PRINCE AND THOUGHT HE WAS ---

Now arrange the circled letters to form the surprise answer, as suggested by the above cartoon.

Print answer here

JUMBLE®

Unscramble these four Jumbles, one letter to each square, to form four ordinary words.

OYMEN

GLUMO

CANOTE

DOTIYD

It would add correctly to begin with. Then, it just fell apart.

Did you buy our extended care program?

THE POORLY MADE ABACUS COULDN'T BE ----

Now arrange the circled letters to form the surprise answer, as suggested by the above cartoon.

Print answer here

142

JUMBLE®

Unscramble these four Jumbles, one letter to each square, to form four ordinary words.

BADIE

GLICO

CAMSTO

WYRIEN

You cast a lovely reflection on the water

This is quite the date. You really know how to treat a girl.

WHEN HE TOOK HIS DATE ON A LITTLE BOAT RIDE, IT WAS ---

Now arrange the circled letters to form the surprise answer, as suggested by the above cartoon.

Print answer " ☐☐☐ " - ☐☐☐☐☐☐☐
here

143

JUMBLE®

Unscramble these four Jumbles, one letter to each square, to form four ordinary words.

KEBIR

OLFRO

LUYFOJ

DUNOBA

Please stop barking! I can't think with all this noise.

BARK BARK BARK BARK BARK BARK BARK BARK BARK

PICK OF THE LITTER

WORKING AT THE DOG KENNEL CAN SOMETIMES BE A ---

Now arrange the circled letters to form the surprise answer, as suggested by the above cartoon.

Print answer here " ◯◯◯◯◯ " ◯◯◯

JUMBLE®

Unscramble these four Jumbles, one letter to each square, to form four ordinary words.

DHICE

CAWTH

HLEWAT

SWYHIM

So, who is Millie and who is Hettie?

Um, I'm not really sure.

THE WITCH HAD TWIN BABY GIRLS, BUT ---

Now arrange the circled letters to form the surprise answer, as suggested by the above cartoon.

Print answer here

  ?

145

JUMBLE®

Unscramble these four Jumbles, one letter to each square, to form four ordinary words.

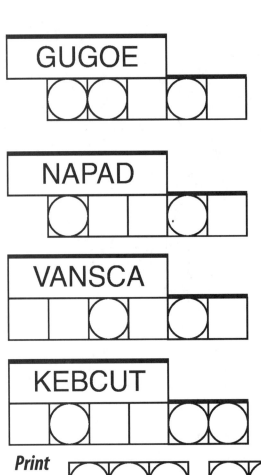

GUGOE

NAPAD

VANSCA

KEBCUT

I thought we were going to run today!

I'll be ready right after this quarter.

HE WANTED TO LEAVE, BUT HE DIDN'T HAVE ENOUGH ----

Now arrange the circled letters to form the surprise answer, as suggested by the above cartoon.

Print answer here

JUMBLE®

Unscramble these four Jumbles, one letter to each square, to form four ordinary words.

VARPO
◯◯ ◯ □□

GINCL
□ ◯◯ □□

DIEMEP
◯□□□ ◯□

TUGBED
□ ◯□□ ◯◯

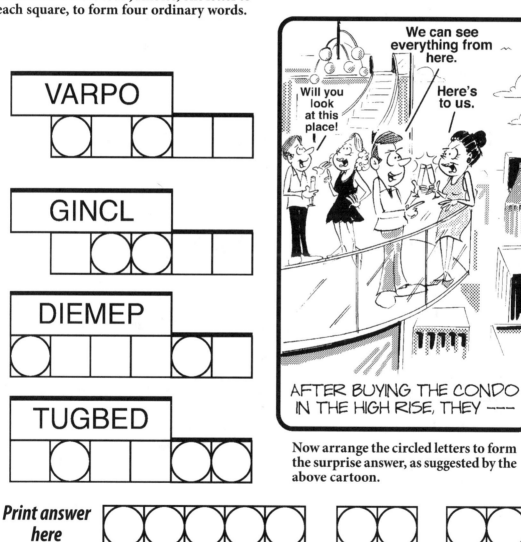

Will you look at this place!

We can see everything from here.

Here's to us.

AFTER BUYING THE CONDO IN THE HIGH RISE, THEY ----

Now arrange the circled letters to form the surprise answer, as suggested by the above cartoon.

Print answer here ◯◯◯◯◯ ◯◯ ◯◯

147

Unscramble these four Jumbles, one letter to each square, to form four ordinary words.

SITJO

TORUG

BIMNEL

SYPBAS

Wow! You're good. I can't even see where the dents were.

We know what we're doing.

HAMMER TIME
AUTO REPAIR

WHEN IT CAME TO REPAIRING CARS, THE AUTO BODY SHOP DID A ---

Now arrange the circled letters to form the surprise answer, as suggested by the above cartoon.

Print answer here ◯◯◯◯ - ◯◯ ◯◯◯

148

JUMBLE®

Unscramble these four Jumbles, one letter to each square, to form four ordinary words.

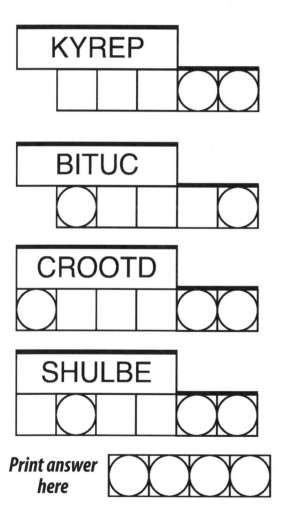

KYREP

BITUC

CROOTD

SHULBE

How can you still be hungry after Thanksgiving dinner?

I've been thinking about a sandwich all night.

HE WANTED TO STOP OVEREATING, BUT HE COULDN'T QUIT ----

Now arrange the circled letters to form the surprise answer, as suggested by the above cartoon.

Print answer here

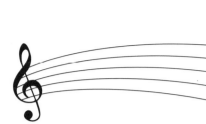

Unscramble these four Jumbles, one letter to each square, to form four ordinary words.

BNEDL

IDOVA

SEHEYC

ARACEM

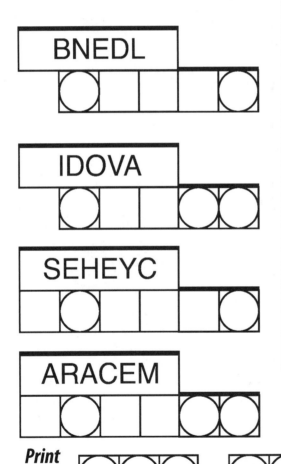

Stop that! What is with you? I thought you like being brushed.

WHEN MEDUSA WAS BITTEN ON THE NECK, SHE HAD A ---

Now arrange the circled letters to form the surprise answer, as suggested by the above cartoon.

Print answer here

JUMBLE®

Unscramble these four Jumbles, one letter to
each square, to form four ordinary words.

GAMOE

PENIT

RULHOY

PUMACS

I'm a big fan! Keep
blitzing those
quarterbacks!
Here's your ticket.

I gotta go.
I'll be late for
the game.

BLTZR

THE FOOTBALL PLAYER
GOT A SPEEDING TICKET
BECAUSE HE WAS ---

Now arrange the circled letters to form
the surprise answer, as suggested by the
above cartoon.

Print answer here

JUMBLE®

Unscramble these four Jumbles, one letter to
each square, to form four ordinary words.

TAFIH

CUEND

PAWNEO

VUDERO

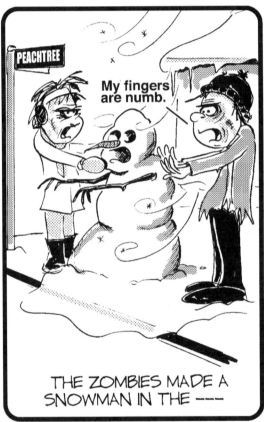

PEACHTREE

My fingers
are numb.

THE ZOMBIES MADE A
SNOWMAN IN THE ----

Now arrange the circled letters to form
the surprise answer, as suggested by the
above cartoon.

Print
answer
here

152

JUMBLE®

Unscramble these four Jumbles, one letter to each square, to form four ordinary words.

TANIG

HIRDT

LANDAS

INDALS

He's an amazing actor.

Such a standout performance.

WHEN JACK NICHOLSON STARRED IN STANLEY KUBRICK'S 1980 FILM, HE WAS A ---

Now arrange the circled letters to form the surprise answer, as suggested by the above cartoon.

Print answer here

153

JUMBLE

Unscramble these four Jumbles, one letter to each square, to form four ordinary words.

SIKKO

XOPYE

UCYNOT

LRAYSA

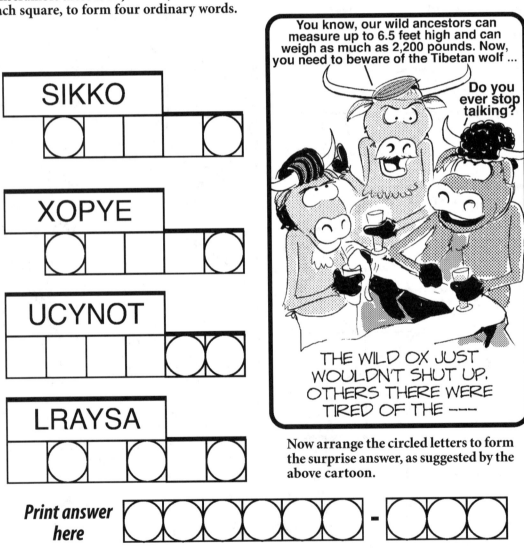

You know, our wild ancestors can measure up to 6.5 feet high and can weigh as much as 2,200 pounds. Now, you need to beware of the Tibetan wolf ...

Do you ever stop talking?

THE WILD OX JUST WOULDN'T SHUT UP. OTHERS THERE WERE TIRED OF THE ----

Now arrange the circled letters to form the surprise answer, as suggested by the above cartoon.

Print answer here ⬡⬡⬡⬡⬡⬡ - ⬡⬡⬡

JUMBLE®

Unscramble these four Jumbles, one letter to
each square, to form four ordinary words.

SIPEO

CHINF

DENMAT

AFORED

WHEN THE COUPLE WENT
SCUBA DIVING ON
VALENTINE'S DAY,
THERE WAS ---

Now arrange the circled letters to form
the surprise answer, as suggested by the
above cartoon.

Print
answer
here

JUMBLE®

Unscramble these four Jumbles, one letter to each square, to form four ordinary words.

LAKAO

RIBTO

MUCSAP

TARTOE

THE PRICES ON THE GRANITE FLOOR TILES WERE ----

Now arrange the circled letters to form the surprise answer, as suggested by the above cartoon.

Print answer here ◯◯◯◯◯ - ◯◯◯◯◯◯◯

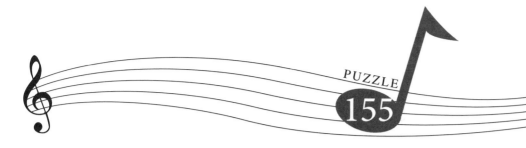

JUMBLE®

Unscramble these four Jumbles, one letter to
each square, to form four ordinary words.

HYNPO

CANHR

TULIFE

AYDAPY

One "I wish" sandwich coming up.

Ham
Turkey
Newt
Frog

Sam's Sandwiches
"My sandwiches are magical!"

I wish I had ordered the submarine.

Hey! What's that?

SHE MADE SUCH A
GOOD WITCH BECAUSE
SHE WAS ---

Now arrange the circled letters to form
the surprise answer, as suggested by the
above cartoon.

Print answer here

157

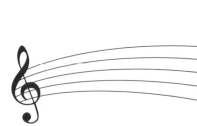

Unscramble these four Jumbles, one letter to
each square, to form four ordinary words.

JYEON

PGARH

PRUBAL

TICILA

You don't
have anyone
to blame but
yourself.

I don't think
I can move.
I'm so
miserable.

HE COMPLAINED ABOUT
HOW FULL HE WAS, AND
HIS WIFE WANTED HIM TO
STOP HIS ---

Now arrange the circled letters to form
the surprise answer, as suggested by the
above cartoon.

Print
answer
here

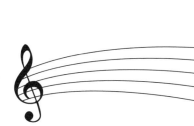

Unscramble these four Jumbles, one letter to each square, to form four ordinary words.

MRYEC

SIPYT

DILCAP

FARIMF

AFTER THE WHITE HOUSE WAS COMPLETED IN 1800, IT HAD A ---

Now arrange the circled letters to form the surprise answer, as suggested by the above cartoon.

Print answer here

JUMBLE®

Unscramble these four Jumbles, one letter to each square, to form four ordinary words.

EVEPE

LENTK

TAVCIE

PANHEP

I'm kind of hungry.

What do you say we split that?

Last slice. Who gets it?

THE POLICEMAN IN THE PIZZA PARLOR WANTED TO ---

Now arrange the circled letters to form the surprise answer, as suggested by the above cartoon.

Print answer here

"   "

JUMBLE®

Unscramble these four Jumbles, one letter to
each square, to form four ordinary words.

SUGIE

POSYU

DOSTEM

VINCOE

Well, that's
not going
to help me
write this
song.

THE ZOMBIE JINGLE
WRITER WAS ---

Now arrange the circled letters to form
the surprise answer, as suggested by the
above cartoon.

Print
answer
here

◯◯ - ◯◯◯◯◯◯◯◯◯◯

JUMBLE®

Unscramble these four Jumbles, one letter to each square, to form four ordinary words.

NARCK

HYLYS

DOEKOH

ESCASC

BEFORE THEY'LL CASH YOUR CHECK, THEY'LL PROBABLY DO THIS.

Now arrange the circled letters to form the surprise answer, as suggested by the above cartoon.

Print answer here ⬭⬭⬭⬭⬭ YOUR ⬭⬭⬭⬭

JUMBLE®

Symphony

Challenger Puzzles

JUMBLE®

Unscramble these six Jumbles, one letter to each square, to form six ordinary words.

HEHRST

ELFENN

YARRIT

KEEBAT

NEDDAW

CLAMBY

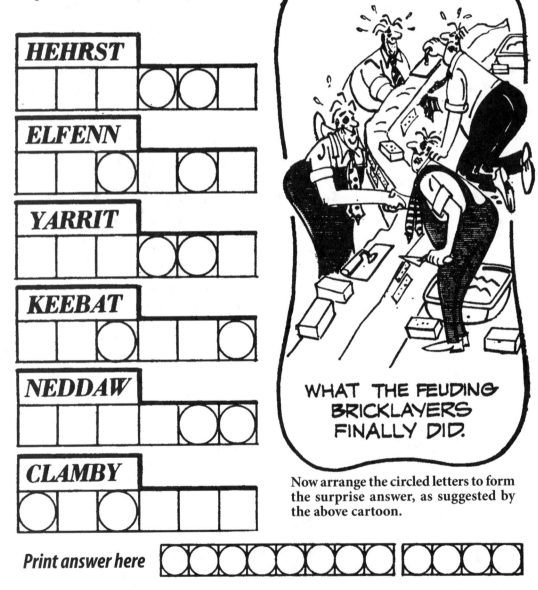

WHAT THE FEUDING BRICKLAYERS FINALLY DID.

Now arrange the circled letters to form the surprise answer, as suggested by the above cartoon.

Print answer here

JUMBLE

Unscramble these six Jumbles, one letter to each square, to form six ordinary words.

FLUWAL

WARIAY

BELUBB

PINGAY

GARNAH

NORGAD

You're looking better

WHAT A HUSBAND WHO HAD RECENTLY BEEN ILL SEEMED TO BE DOING.

Now arrange the circled letters to form the surprise answer, as suggested by the above cartoon.

Print answer here

165

JUMBLE®

Unscramble these six Jumbles, one letter to each square, to form six ordinary words.

DYNKIL

YIELDE

THORCC

LOWALT

RAMPHE

CLAMIE

WHY NEWBORN KITTENS WALK SOFTLY.

Now arrange the circled letters to form the surprise answer, as suggested by the above cartoon.

Print answer here **THEY CAN'T** ⭕⭕⭕⭕⭕⭕ ⭕⭕⭕⭕

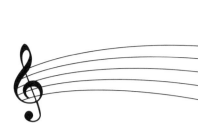

JUMBLE®

Unscramble these six Jumbles, one letter to
each square, to form six ordinary words.

COYTUR

HEEBAD

TISSAD

DEAGAN

NOSHET

ORDINO

THE FARMER RAISED HIS
BOY TO BE A BOOTBLACK
BECAUSE HE WANTED
TO DO THIS.

Now arrange the circled letters to form
the surprise answer, as suggested by
the above cartoon.

Print
answer
here   MAKE ◯◯◯ WHILE THE ◯◯◯◯ ◯◯◯◯◯◯◯

JUMBLE®

Unscramble these six Jumbles, one letter to each square, to form six ordinary words.

LINCEY

DORRIT

REMMEB

HESKAN

GAHOME

LAASSI

This'll make you well!

HOW A WESTERN DOCTOR MIGHT GIVE YOU AN INOCULATION.

Now arrange the circled letters to form the surprise answer, as suggested by the above cartoon.

Print answer here

WITH HIS ⟨◯◯◯◯⟩ ⟨◯◯◯◯◯◯⟩

JUMBLE®

Unscramble these six Jumbles, one letter to
each square, to form six ordinary words.

FICTEN

INTOOM

WRALEY

HOGUNE

PARULL

SILCHE

WHAT TO GET WHEN
YOUR DIET FAILS.

Now arrange the circled letters to form
the surprise answer, as suggested by
the above cartoon.

Print answer here

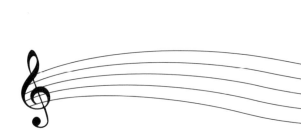

Unscramble these six Jumbles, one letter to each square, to form six ordinary words.

ZEFRYN

NUGHAT

MISOGE

JELIAD

GRATTE

PARTUB

THIS IS CERTAINLY THE PERFECT SQUARE OF THE CENTURY!

Now arrange the circled letters to form the surprise answer, as suggested by the above cartoon.

Print answer here

170

JUMBLE®

Unscramble these six Jumbles, one letter to
each square, to form six ordinary words.

YETTIN

GLINTE

ROHRRO

GRIBED

THACCY

MIRADS

WHAT YOU GENERALLY
GET BEFORE YOU DO
THE LAUNDRY.

Now arrange the circled letters to form
the surprise answer, as suggested by
the above cartoon.

**Print answer
here** **THE** ⬡⬡⬡⬡⬡⬡⬡ ⬡⬡⬡⬡⬡

JUMBLE®

Unscramble these six Jumbles, one letter to each square, to form six ordinary words.

YIMWAD

DEXENP

BRENAT

TYNTOK

TORTOG

DISPUT

WHAT A HUSBAND WHO WON'T STAND FOR HIS WIFE'S EXTRAVAGANCE WILL PROBABLY HAVE TO DO.

Now arrange the circled letters to form the surprise answer, as suggested by the above cartoon.

Print answer here

IT

172

JUMBLE®

Unscramble these six Jumbles, one letter to
each square, to form six ordinary words.

MUPTIE

PUNCOO

OCTIXE

SHOIBY

DUSARI

LOSTID

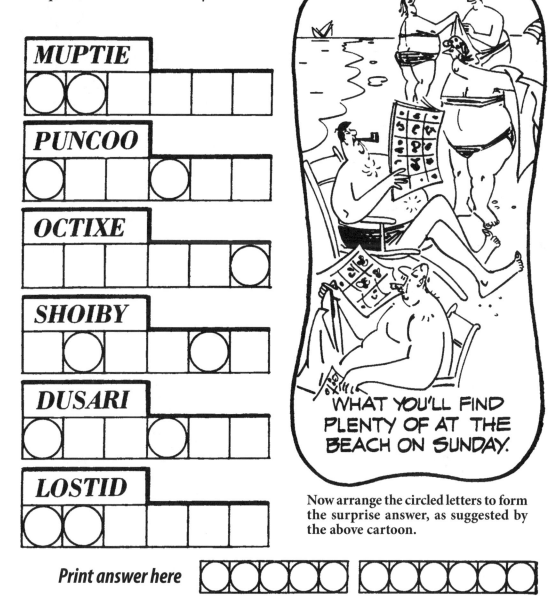

WHAT YOU'LL FIND
PLENTY OF AT THE
BEACH ON SUNDAY.

Now arrange the circled letters to form
the surprise answer, as suggested by
the above cartoon.

Print answer here

JUMBLE®

Unscramble these six Jumbles, one letter to each square, to form six ordinary words.

TAFRYC

NOITUG

DIFELD

PULOEC

XELUED

RAYSOV

What is her deal tonight?

I just fed you. Your diaper is dry. Give us a break...

AFTER BEING AWAKENED BY THE BABY SO MANY TIMES THAT THEY COULDN'T GET ANY SLEEP, THE PARENTS SAID THIS.

Now arrange the circled letters to form the surprise answer, as suggested by the above cartoon.

Print answer here

174

JUMBLE®

Unscramble these six Jumbles, one letter to
each square, to form six ordinary words.

NATCIT

MOYRAR

SUNGIE

OPSERN

WEENPH

NINETT

I figured he'd win again.

Despite the elements, he makes it two in a row!

SINKING THE PUTT AT
THE BRITISH OPEN IN A
DOWNPOUR MADE
HIM THE ---

Now arrange the circled letters to form
the surprise answer, as suggested by
the above cartoon.

Print answer here

" ◯◯◯◯◯◯◯ " ◯◯◯◯◯◯◯

JUMBLE®

Unscramble these six Jumbles, one letter to each square, to form six ordinary words.

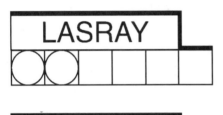
LASRAY

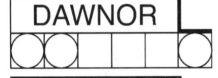
DAWNOR

PUBTAR

THIREM

LOVINI

CRONEE

He's coming along fine. You can take him out for a ride soon.

AFTER GETTING INJURED, THE HORSE WAS NOW IN ----

Now arrange the circled letters to form the surprise answer, as suggested by the above cartoon.

Print answer here

JUMBLE®

Unscramble these six Jumbles, one letter to each square, to form six ordinary words.

CANGEL

DAPTUE

DARUNO

WEERPT

WHERDS

RIFMON

Morning, Pete.

Morning! Your carrots look great!

1A

1B

THE RABBITS LIVED IN A ---

Now arrange the circled letters to form the surprise answer, as suggested by the above cartoon.

Print answer here

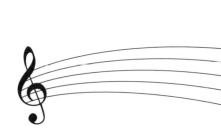

Unscramble these six Jumbles, one letter to each square, to form six ordinary words.

LASNOM

TARGEY

TALNEY

WASYLA

TINVAY

RABPUL

You do know that PowerPoint doesn't mean poking your finger harder, don't you?

I don't find any of this remotely funny.

How many professors does it take to screw in an LED?

XYZ, sir.

WHEN THEY PICKED ON THE NEWEST PROFESSOR, THEY BECAME ----

Now arrange the circled letters to form the surprise answer, as suggested by the above cartoon.

Print answer here

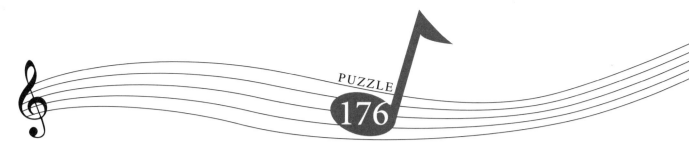

JUMBLE®

Unscramble these six Jumbles, one letter to each square, to form six ordinary words.

DARISU

INROGI

CHKEST

CLIFNH

REHLAB

ESTERO

THE SMART
SWIMMER
HAD THESE.

Now arrange the circled letters to form the surprise answer, as suggested by the above cartoon.

Print answer here

JUMBLE®

Unscramble these six Jumbles, one letter to
each square, to form six ordinary words.

MESSEA

NIVSAH

TROMSY

AMEWOD

REPLUP

DORWAN

I hear that the trout fishing is great here.

Yep! People have been lining up to fish here all month.

Fish Here!
Day Pass $5
Month Pass $25

WHEN HE STARTED
CHARGING PEOPLE TO
FISH IN HIS CREEK, IT
CREATED A ----

Now arrange the circled letters to form
the surprise answer, as suggested by
the above cartoon.

Print answer here

JUMBLE®

Unscramble these six Jumbles, one letter to each square, to form six ordinary words.

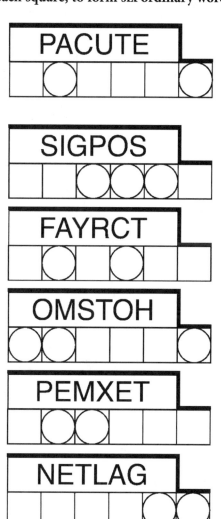

PACUTE

SIGPOS

FAYRCT

OMSTOH

PEMXET

NETLAG

AFTER GETTING IN THE 10 ITEMS OR LESS LINE, THE CUSTOMER WAS READY TO ---

Now arrange the circled letters to form the surprise answer, as suggested by the above cartoon.

Print answer here

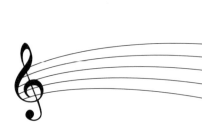

Unscramble these six Jumbles, one letter to each square, to form six ordinary words.

PYMRUG

THECKS

BENLIB

OFICAS

RURPES

OVITEL

This is a classic setup. You're not going to find a better deal. What do you say?

I saw the same kit at Levon's Drums with double bass drums and it cost less.

$2,000

HE DIDN'T BUY THE DRUM SET BECAUSE HE WANTED ----

Now arrange the circled letters to form the surprise answer, as suggested by the above cartoon.

Print answer here

◯◯◯◯ ◯◯◯◯◯ FOR ◯◯◯ ◯◯◯◯◯

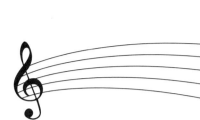

PUZZLE 180

Unscramble these six Jumbles, one letter to each square, to form six ordinary words.

PANPEH

DREEGN

UMENIM

CLAPAE

OIRCIN

LESGUD

I didn't want butter on this.

I'll call the attendant.

AFTER BEING SERVED A BAGEL IN FIRST CLASS, THE PASSENGER WANTED ---

Now arrange the circled letters to form the surprise answer, as suggested by the above cartoon.

Print answer here

" ☐☐☐☐☐ " ☐☐☐☐☐☐ ☐☐☐☐☐☐☐

Answers

1. **Jumbles:** PUDGY BUMPY EGOISM FINERY
   Answer: What it was when the doctor said, "This won't hurt"—AN "M.D." PROMISE (empty promise)

2. **Jumbles:** MAXIM WAFER MAGPIE THRASH
   Answer: The waiter finally comes to this—HIM WHO WAITS

3. **Jumbles:** BORAX AFIRE FOMENT BARROW
   Answer: He was the type of man some women take to—and also this—FROM

4. **Jumbles:** GIANT AUGUR FORKED SNITCH
   Answer: What they called the star of the monster show—A STAGE "FRIGHT"

5. **Jumbles:** YOUNG IDIOT DREDGE VANDAL
   Answer: A beauty salon is a place where this might happen—THE LIVING GO TO "DYE"

6. **Jumbles:** BYLAW GRIME KIDNAP DOUBLE
   Answer: What a game of golf sometimes is—A GOOD WALK RUINED

7. **Jumbles:** FEVER BASIN CASKET GOBLET
   Answer: The best thing to save for old age—ONESELF

8. **Jumbles:** SYLPH TYPED MUSLIN HOURLY
   Answer: What you have to have lots of in order to open up the door to success—PUSH & PULL

9. **Jumbles:** CROUP BARGE ADJUST EULOGY
   Answer: How he felt about feeling bad—GOOD

10. **Jumbles:** GUIDE SANDY NINETY FLURRY
    Answer: What the unhappy pig was—"DIS-GRUNT-LED"

11. **Jumbles:** DRAWL EIGHT DEPICT NAUSEA
    Answer: If you're going to act like a skunk just make sure nobody does this—GETS WIND OF IT

12. **Jumbles:** YOKEL PIVOT NIBBLE GAMBLE
    Answer: What some college students major in—"ALIBI-OLOGY"

13. **Jumbles:** GLOVE CLEFT CACTUS FEDORA
    Answer: What the runner's diet consisted of, naturally—FAST FOOD

14. **Jumbles:** HABIT PAUSE HARBOR GENDER
    Answer: What those snobbish members of the horsey set thought they were—A BREED APART

15. **Jumbles:** SOOTY OAKEN RATHER MUSTER
    Answer: What you might get from astronomers—"NO MORE STARS"

16. **Jumbles:** VENOM TOOTH BYGONE MOTION
    Answer: How those folks who enjoyed eating grits sang—IN "HOMINY" (harmony)

17. **Jumbles:** PRONE HUSKY SMOKER ELEVEN
    Answer: "What do you think of that poet?"—I'VE SEEN "VERSE"

18. **Jumbles:** SAUTE BRAND REALTY COUSIN
    Answer: What he did when she asked him to buy her that expensive perfume—HE "A-SCENTED"

19. **Jumbles:** VAPOR FRAME NUMBER STYLUS
    Answer: Why they called for the chimney sweep—IT WAS THE "FLUE" SEASON

20. **Jumbles:** HUMAN BRASS CUDDLE TEAPOT
    Answer: What he was when he saw that tree trunk right in the middle of the road—"STUMPED"

21. **Jumbles:** MOTIF WOVEN PARLOR FLORAL
    Answer: How he felt after eating too many pancakes—"WAFFLE" (awful)

22. **Jumbles:** GRIPE MOUTH GYPSUM SUPERB
    Answer: What small sled dogs are called—"MUSH" PUPPIES

23. **Jumbles:** LIGHT PRIOR CORNEA GUIDED
    Answer: What the card game at the oil field must have been—"RIGGED"

24. **Jumbles:** VALVE CHEEK RABBIT BETRAY
    Answer: How they greeted each other at the cardiologists' annual shindig—HEARTILY

25. **Jumbles:** TRAIT FENCE EXPOSE GARLIC
    Answer: What firewood used to be—FREE FOR THE "AXING"

26. **Jumbles:** EJECT SAVOR CIPHER PARISH
    Answer: Sounds like a fish who thinks he's a bird—A PERCH ON A PERCH

27. **Jumbles:** PIKER FRAUD SOLACE NOTIFY
    Answer: The best way to watch calories, if you want to lose weight—FROM A DISTANCE

28. **Jumbles:** EVOKE SMACK POWDER NEPHEW
    Answer: What the helicopter tycoon decided to get for himself—NEW CHOPPERS

29. **Jumbles:** QUEER DOUSE TYRANT HERESY
    Answer: What they said about the angry governor—WHAT A "STATE" HE'S IN!

30. **Jumbles:** HOUSE NAÏVE VIRTUE QUAVER
    Answer: What Junior was when Mom accused him of breaking her favorite urn—"E-VASE-IVE"

31. **Jumbles:** ODIUM COACH TYPIST INDUCE
    Answer: What the hash slinger knew how to do—DISH IT OUT

32. **Jumbles:** JOINT ROACH PAGODA CYMBAL
    Answer: What "diplomacy" sometimes turns out to be—"MAD POLICY"

33. **Jumbles:** DINER NIECE UPROAR COUPON
    Answer: How the hotel room clerk appeared—"PREOCCUPIED"

34. **Jumbles:** PROBE USURY STRONG MUTTON
    Answer: How he worked his way "down" in the world—FROM BOTTOMS "UP"

35. **Jumbles:** QUIRE GUMBO LAYOFF CROUCH
    Answer: Did the X-rated movie make any money?—"BARE-LY"

36. **Jumbles:** WAGON PORGY BOUNCE WIZARD
    Answer: What boys do when they grow up—GROW "DOWN"

37. **Jumbles:** LANKY AWASH HUNGRY DETACH
    Answer: What sort of existence did that crapshooter lead?—A "SHAKY" ONE

38. **Jumbles:** KNELL FINNY IMPORT GLANCE
    Answer: There's usually a fine for parking in any spot that's this—FINE FOR PARKING

39. **Jumbles:** DERBY COLON NAPKIN SIPHON
    Answer: What a worker who watches the clock generally remains—ONE OF THE "HANDS"

40. **Jumbles:** SINGE BROOD LAGOON MUSCLE
    Answer: What a good book usually is—"BOUND" TO SELL

41. **Jumbles:** KHAKI HARPY QUEASY TUMULT
    Answer: What a belly laugh is—A "MIRTH" QUAKE

42. **Jumbles:** PLAIT SUITE INJECT PASTRY
    Answer: The most brutal aspect of boxing these days—THE PRICE OF SEATS

43. **Jumbles:** NUDGE SOUSE HEARTH BOUGHT
    Answer: How you have to pay for some kinds of plastic surgery—THROUGH THE NOSE

44. **Jumbles:** SIXTY ENVOY MANIAC ALKALI
    Answer: A man who takes you into his "confidence" often does this afterwards—JUST TAKES YOU IN

45. **Jumbles:** SNARL SCARF COERCE FUNGUS
    Answer: Political candidates often stay on the fence in order to avoid giving this—"OF-FENSE"

46. **Jumbles:** CURIO ANISE DENTAL STYMIE
Answer: What a letter carrier might be advised to wear—
A SUIT OF "MAIL"

47. **Jumbles:** VERVE PATIO SICKEN CASHEW
Answer: Some college kids who spend too much time with a pigskin sometimes fail to get this—A SHEEPSKIN

48. **Jumbles:** ABBOT PROXY INFLUX DAMASK
Answer: What a chip on the shoulder usually is—
JUST PLAIN "BARK"

49. **Jumbles:** KNACK CUBIC CABANA PURITY
Answer: What most of the chiropractor's income came from—"BACK" PAY

50. **Jumbles:** JOLLY KINKY CATCHY FIRING
Answer: A bachelor prefers to remain single, while others would this—"KNOT"

51. **Jumbles:** IDIOM TAWNY ICEBOX SHERRY
Answer: What some people give when they lose their inhibitions—EXHIBITIONS

52. **Jumbles:** POPPY BERTH RARELY MEMOIR
Answer: How he arranged the salmon eggs—"ROE" BY "ROE"

53. **Jumbles:** KEYED WINCE INVITE BICEPS
Answer: What kind of a game is croquet?—A "WICKET" ONE

54. **Jumbles:** MURKY BARON EXHORT RADIUS
Answer: What a bridge player has to learn how to do—
TAKE IT ON THE SHIN

55. **Jumbles:** NERVY RURAL PODIUM BRANDY
Answer: What the counterfeiter wanted—MONEY "BAD"

56. **Jumbles:** EATEN GOOSE VERMIN EYELID
Answer: What some people do when they hold a conversation—NEVER LET GO

57. **Jumbles:** VOCAL PUTTY NESTLE MODERN
Answer: A small boy might wear out everything, including this—HIS PARENTS

58. **Jumbles:** NATAL OUTDO PIGEON TOUCHY
Answer: What form of locomotion is drag racing?—
A "LOCO" NOTION

59. **Jumbles:** GUMMY SURLY HEALTH GOVERN
Answer: The "one that got away" would have been bigger if the fisherman had this—LONGER ARMS

60. **Jumbles:** LARVA VISOR POTTER COLUMN
Answer: Some men can't be trusted too far—or this—
TOO NEAR

61. **Jumbles:** NIPPY COWER NATURE POORLY
Answer: A calculator is a device used by these—
PEOPLE WHO COUNT

62. **Jumbles:** CRAWL HANDY JUNGLE RATION
Answer: Where you might go in order to make yourself more attractive—OUT OF YOUR "WEIGH"

63. **Jumbles:** JEWEL FRANC BOTHER FEUDAL
Answer: If you're not careful about lending an ear you might get this—IT CHEWED OFF

64. **Jumbles:** SILKY VISTA CALICO ENTAIL
Answer: A "still" is an apparatus that makes many people this—"NOISY"

65. **Jumbles:** RAVEN MOCHA INFECT OPPOSE
Answer: "Can you tell me what Napoleon's origin was?"—
"OF CORS-I-CAN"

66. **Jumbles:** DOILY RAJAH MAKEUP TRYING
Answer: What peroxide might do—TURN HER HEAD

67. **Jumbles:** APART WHOSE IMPUGN TAMPER
Answer: Some people with the gift of gab never know when to do this—WRAP IT UP

68. **Jumbles:** SQUAB TWICE MAINLY FABRIC
Answer: That snobbish skunk was unpopular because he was always putting on this—SUCH AWFUL "AIRS"

69. **Jumbles:** BIPED IMBUE TUXEDO MANAGE
Answer: What to do when you have the feeling you want to spend more than you can afford—NIP IT IN THE "BUD-GET"

70. **Jumbles:** PHOTO FAMED DEFACE HALLOW
Answer: The best thing to have in a heated discussion—
A COOL HEAD

71. **Jumbles:** NUTTY WHEEL OMELET BABOON
Answer: What happens when you slip on thin ice?—
YOUR BOTTOM GETS "THAW"

72. **Jumbles:** KITTY LOGIC JOBBER ABACUS
Answer: What two wrongs sometimes actually do make—
A "RIOT"

73. **Jumbles:** MILKY GAVEL SONATA TIMING
Answer: He had the self-control to give up drinking and smoking but not the self-control to give up this—
TALKING ABOUT IT

74. **Jumbles:** MINUS SCOUR VOYAGE PURPLE
Answer: If it sounds like a "whine," it's probably a complaint that comes from this—SOUR GRAPES

75. **Jumbles:** DOUSE IDIOT ABSORB SHEKEL
Answer: What a self-employed person is never apt to do—
DISLIKE THE BOSS

76. **Jumbles:** KNOWN HAZEL EQUITY COUGAR
Answer: That next-door neighbor who's always borrowing your stuff will take anything from you except this—A HINT

77. **Jumbles:** GOUGE QUILT MELODY SEETHE
Answer: What a mean man who would steal candy from a baby is—A HEEL WITHOUT A "SOUL"

78. **Jumbles:** TYING NOTCH MISUSE VALISE
Answer: What the boy snake said to the girl snake—
GIVE US A HISS

79. **Jumbles:** CAKED REBEL BARREN DISOWN
Answer: A pessimist is always good for this—BAD NEWS

80. **Jumbles:** VODKA THEME WILLOW POCKET
Answer: When little Raymond Romano was born on 12-21-57, everybody—LOVED HIM

81. **Jumbles:** JOIST DAFFY SCULPT PIMPLE
Answer: The quarterback did this after being presented with the endorsement deal—PASSED IT UP

82. **Jumbles:** VERGE WRING BATTER SIMILE
Answer: Valley Ave. in Bangor is a—"MAINE" STREET

83. **Jumbles:** PURGE UPEND ACCORD GENIUS
Answer: She liked seeing all the presents, but she really liked everyone's—PRESENCE

84. **Jumbles:** SORRY FENCE VALLEY OUTFIT
Answer: After watching so many horror movies in a row, they were this—"FEAR-FULL"

85. **Jumbles:** MUNCH IDIOT HEDGE UNWIND
Answer: Dr. Frankenstein put a faulty brain in his monster, but the monster—DIDN'T MIND

86. **Jumbles:** BLOCK RANCH NEARLY WISDOM
Answer: Presiding over 100 trials was this for the judge—
A BENCHMARK

87. **Jumbles:** SPOIL AWAKE TANNED CLOUDY
Answer: After tasting his perfectly cooked, medium-rare steak, the customer said this—WELL DONE

88. **Jumbles:** NOVEL OCTET LESSON PARADE
Answer: As the owner of the most successful sandwich shop in town, he was this—ON A ROLL

89. **Jumbles:** TIGHT BLISS BAKING RESUME
Answer: Smokey got lost in the woods after he lost this—
HIS BEARINGS

90. **Jumbles:** PILOT KAZOO SHRUNK LATELY
Answer: When a young Elvis topped the music charts in April 1957, some parents were—ALL SHOOK UP

91. **Jumbles:** TIGER CLUNG NUMBER GENIUS
Answer: The marathon winner's favorite part of owning his store was—RUNNING IT

185

92. **Jumbles:** FLOOR GLOAT GLANCE IMPOSE
Answer: Before the wedding ceremony, the husband-to-be was—GROOMING

93. **Jumbles:** VOUCH WEARY BOLDLY UPBEAT
Answer: The bird decided to steal the diamond necklace because he felt he was—ABOVE THE LAW

94. **Jumbles:** ELUDE RHYME INFECT BURLAP
Answer: Whether or not the zoo's new pachyderm was from Africa or Asia was—"IRRELEPHANT"

95. **Jumbles:** PIANO MONEY POETIC FABRIC
Answer: The business owned by the mom and dad was a—PARENT COMPANY

96. **Jumbles:** GIVEN BUNCH INJURY ADJUST
Answer: They installed solar panels on their house because it was a—BRIGHT IDEA

97. **Jumbles:** WEAVE VALET BUTTER AFFORD
Answer: The twins missed their flight because they were—"TWO" LATE

98. **Jumbles:** GAUGE MESSY VANISH HERMIT
Answer: When they looked for a place to build their new home, they were—"SITE"-SEEING

99. **Jumbles:** CRIMP CROAK DETACH ROCKET
Answer: Dinner at the expensive steakhouse was—A RARE TREAT

100. **Jumbles:** DOUBT CIVIC PAPAYA HOMELY
Answer: The tiger's twin brother was a—COPYCAT

101. **Jumbles:** THIEF IMAGE KOSHER ICONIC
Answer: When she bought her husband a fancy new recliner, he promised to—"CHAIR-ISH" IT

102. **Jumbles:** MACAW FRAME ELEVEN EQUITY
Answer: The baby monkey was born in the—FAMILY TREE

103. **Jumbles:** EMCEE FULLY JABBER EMBARK
Answer: They didn't like working with the obnoxious tree cutter because he was a—"LUMBERJERK"

104. **Jumbles:** STUNT SCOUR EMBLEM WAITER
Answer: They rented an apartment on that particular road because they were—STREET SMART

105. **Jumbles:** SLASH ERUPT ROTATE POUNCE
Answer: They went snorkeling to—"SEE" TURTLES

106. **Jumbles:** AGAIN OMEGA DISOWN ENTOMB
Answer: When he realized that their golden retriever wasn't in the backyard, he said—"DOG-GONE-IT"

107. **Jumbles:** PRANK AVOID DILUTE ENGAGE
Answer: H.G. Wells' concept to write a book about a time machine was a—NOVEL IDEA

108. **Jumbles:** GLORY DRINK SPLINT ZENITH
Answer: The resemblance between the pitchers was—STRIKING

109. **Jumbles:** GRUNT OPERA UNJUST ENGULF
Answer: When he asked her if she wanted a new mink coat, she said—"FUR" SURE

110. **Jumbles:** WINDY DRIFT SLEEPY VIABLE
Answer: The hawk saw the whole incident, thanks to her—BIRD'S-EYE VIEW

111. **Jumbles:** PRIOR GUEST EXOTIC MATTER
Answer: The puppy that shredded the morning newspaper was a—"TEAR-IER"

112. **Jumbles:** GUESS BRIBE CELERY UNPACK
Answer: The star of the new "Deer Hunter" show was beginning to—EARN BIG BUCKS

113. **Jumbles:** DROLL ABIDE LAGOON FATHOM
Answer: The fleet of giant octopuses was an—ARMADA

114. **Jumbles:** RIVER STAND VIOLET RELENT
Answer: Bifocals were becoming as popular as Ben Franklin—ENVISIONED

115. **Jumbles:** BOSSY UNITY RODENT RUNNER
Answer: Camping during the thunderstorm was—"IN-TENTS"

116. **Jumbles:** GRUFF KNIFE RITUAL PHOBIA
Answer: Elvis Presley's new custom-made suit was—FIT FOR A KING

117. **Jumbles:** BOGUS GLINT FIASCO AVIARY
Answer: The weatherman bought the new fishing pole—FOR CASTING

118. **Jumbles:** ABYSS PLANK UNCORK FROZEN
Answer: When Sinatra gave the young singer advice, he—SPOKE FRANKLY

119. **Jumbles:** GLADE PROVE PLIGHT PANTRY
Answer: He couldn't wait to propose to his girlfriend in person, so he—GAVE HER A RING

120. **Jumbles:** FENCE UNCLE SHRILL INSIST
Answer: The Helsinki marathon ended at the—"FINNISH" LINE

121. **Jumbles:** HIKER MUDDY DELUGE IMPACT
Answer: When it came to getting new business, the musical instrument store—DRUMMED IT UP

122. **Jumbles:** BLANK RODEO UPDATE GOSSIP
Answer: When the P.A. system broke, he had to become a—LOUD SPEAKER

123. **Jumbles:** PARCH ADMIT TRUANT PEWTER
Answer: The army base had a softball team and the general was the—TEAM CAPTAIN

124. **Jumbles:** FEVER VAULT DAINTY FEWEST
Answer: When the coach took him out of the game, the starting pitcher was—RELIEVED

125. **Jumbles:** BARON MESSY POSTAL RITUAL
Answer: After his plastic surgery, Donald Duck had—BILL PAYMENTS

126. **Jumbles:** KUDOS BRING LAWYER MOSAIC
Answer: He promised to give up cigarettes, but he was just—BLOWING SMOKE

127. **Jumbles:** RAINY VALID ORATOR VELVET
Answer: He practiced the high jump—OVER AND OVER

128. **Jumbles:** CREPT MUSHY FITTED CAUCUS
Answer: After arriving late, the symphony conductor—FACED THE MUSIC

129. **Jumbles:** FLANK SOUPY RANCID SHREWD
Answer: After the collision at home plate, the player's mother was glad he was—SAFE AND SOUND

130. **Jumbles:** BLAST RELIC WINERY FLANGE
Answer: He wanted to practice with his new clubs, so he planned to—SWING BY LATER

131. **Jumbles:** TAKEN TRUMP COBALT CALMLY
Answer: The cattle rancher wanted to stock up, so he went to the—BULL MARKET

132. **Jumbles:** PRIZE AGAIN TUMBLE NEEDLE
Answer: He tried to build a working teleporter, but his plans never—MATERIALIZED

133. **Jumbles:** ONION SWIFT DOCKET WRENCH
Answer: Asked if their band would score, Pete Townshend and Roger Daltrey said—WHO KNOWS

134. **Jumbles:** GLAZE RIGID PROFIT NEGATE
Answer: She thought that winning the $1,000 in the raffle was a—GRAND PRIZE

135. **Jumbles:** DECAY QUILT ENGINE POUNCE
Answer: After a hectic day, he was happy to have this to eat his slice of pizza—"PIECE" AND QUIET

136. **Jumbles:** CELLO ROYAL UNFOLD WINDOW
Answer: After the circus ended, some of the performers liked to—CLOWN AROUND

137. **Jumbles:** AVIAN CARGO DIMWIT MUSCLE
Answer: She wanted her sister to find a guy to go out with, so she gave her a—MANDATE

138. **Jumbles:** IGLOO FLUID CHOSEN DRIVEL
Answer: Casper's date for the Halloween party was his—"GHOUL"-FRIEND

139. **Jumbles:** HUMUS AGENT DECEIT GROGGY
Answer: Everyone loved the prince and thought he was—CHARMING

140. **Jumbles:** MONEY MOGUL OCTANE ODDITY
Answer: The poorly made abacus couldn't be—COUNTED ON

141. **Jumbles:** ABIDE LOGIC MASCOT WINERY
Answer: When he took his date on a little boat ride, it was—"ROW"-MANTIC

142. **Jumbles:** BIKER FLOOR JOYFUL ABOUND
Answer: Working at the dog kennel can sometimes be a—"RUFF" JOB

143. **Jumbles:** CHIDE WATCH WEALTH WHIMSY
Answer: The witch had twin baby girls, but—WHICH WAS WHICH?

144. **Jumbles:** GOUGE PANDA CANVAS BUCKET
Answer: He wanted to leave, but he didn't have enough—GET-UP-AND-GO

145. **Jumbles:** VAPOR CLING IMPEDE BUDGET
Answer: After buying the condo in the high rise, they—LIVED IT UP

146. **Jumbles:** JOIST GROUT NIMBLE BYPASS
Answer: When it came to repairing cars, the auto body shop did a—BANG-UP JOB

147. **Jumbles:** PERKY CUBIT DOCTOR BUSHEL
Answer: He wanted to stop overeating, but he couldn't quit—COLD TURKEY

148. **Jumbles:** BLEND AVOID CHEESY CAMERA
Answer: When Medusa was bitten on the neck, she had a—BAD HAIR DAY

149. **Jumbles:** OMEGA INEPT HOURLY CAMPUS
Answer: The football player got a speeding ticket because he was—RUSHING

150. **Jumbles:** FAITH DUNCE WEAPON DEVOUR
Answer: The zombies made a snowman in the—DEAD OF WINTER

151. **Jumbles:** GIANT THIRD SANDAL ISLAND
Answer: When Jack Nicholson starred in Stanley Kubrick's 1980 film, he was a—SHINING STAR

152. **Jumbles:** KIOSK EPOXY COUNTY SALARY
Answer: The wild ox just wouldn't shut up. Others there were tired of the—YAKETY-YAK

153. **Jumbles:** POISE FINCH TANDEM FEDORA
Answer: When the couple went scuba diving on Valentine's Day, there was—DEEP AFFECTION

154. **Jumbles:** KOALA ORBIT CAMPUS ROTATE
Answer: The prices on the granite floor tiles were—ROCK-BOTTOM

155. **Jumbles:** PHONY RANCH FUTILE PAYDAY
Answer: She made such a good witch because she was—CRAFTY

156. **Jumbles:** ENJOY GRAPH BURLAP ITALIC
Answer: He complained about how full he was, and his wife wanted him to stop his—BELLYACHING

157. **Jumbles:** MERCY TIPSY PLACID AFFIRM
Answer: After the White House was completed in 1800, it had a—FIRST FAMILY

158. **Jumbles:** PEEVE KNELT ACTIVE HAPPEN
Answer: The policeman in the pizza parlor wanted to—KEEP THE "PIECE"

159. **Jumbles:** GUISE SOUPY MODEST NOVICE
Answer: The zombie jingle writer was—DE-COMPOSING

160. **Jumbles:** CRANK SHYLY HOOKED ACCESS
Answer: Before they'll cash your check, they'll probably do this—CHECK YOUR CASH

161. **Jumbles:** THRESH FENNEL RARITY BETAKE DAWNED CYMBAL
Answer: What the feuding bricklayers finally did—CEMENTED TIES

162. **Jumbles:** LAWFUL AIRWAY BUBBLE PAYING HANGAR DRAGON
Answer: What a husband who had recently been ill seemed to be doing—HOLDING UP WELL

163. **Jumbles:** KINDLY EYELID CROTCH TALLOW HAMPER MALICE
Answer: Why newborn kittens walk softly—THEY CAN'T HARDLY WALK

164. **Jumbles:** OUTCRY BEHEAD SADIST AGENDA HONEST INDOOR
Answer: The farmer raised his boy to be a bootblack because he wanted to do this—MAKE HAY WHILE THE SON SHINES

165. **Jumbles:** NICELY TORRID MEMBER SHAKEN HOMAGE ASSAIL
Answer: How a Western doctor might give you an inoculation—WITH HIS SICK SHOOTER

166. **Jumbles:** INFECT MOTION LAWYER ENOUGH PLURAL CHISEL
Answer: What to get when your diet fails—ALTERATIONS

167. **Jumbles:** FRENZY NAUGHT EGOISM JAILED TARGET ABRUPT
Answer: This is certainly the perfect square of the century!—TEN THOUSAND

168. **Jumbles:** ENTITY TINGLE HORROR BRIDGE CATCHY DISARM
Answer: What you generally get before you do the laundry—THE CLOTHES DIRTY

169. **Jumbles:** MIDWAY EXPEND BANTER KNOTTY GROTTO STUPID
Answer: What a husband who won't stand for his wife's extravagance will probably have to do—TAKE IT SITTING DOWN

170. **Jumbles:** IMPUTE COUPON EXOTIC BOYISH RADIUS STOLID
Answer: What you'll find plenty of at the beach on Sunday—COMIC STRIPS

171. **Jumbles:** CRAFTY FIDDLE DELUXE OUTING COUPLE SAVORY
Answer: After being awakened by the baby so many times that they couldn't get any sleep, the parents said this—FOR CRYING OUT LOUD

172. **Jumbles:** INTACT GENIUS NEPHEW ARMORY PERSON INTENT
Answer: Sinking the putt at the British Open in a downpour made him the—"RAINING" CHAMPION

173. **Jumbles:** SALARY ABRUPT VIOLIN ONWARD HERMIT ENCORE
Answer: After getting injured, the horse was now in—STABLE CONDITION

174. **Jumbles:** GLANCE AROUND SHREWD UPDATE PEWTER INFORM
Answer: The rabbits lived in a—GARDEN APARTMENT

175. **Jumbles:** SALMON NEATLY VANITY GYRATE ALWAYS BURLAP
Answer: When they picked on the newest professor, they became—BRAIN TEASERS

176. **Jumbles:** RADIUS SKETCH HERBAL ORIGIN FLINCH STEREO
Answer: The smart swimmer had these—STROKES OF GENIUS

177. **Jumbles:** SESAME STORMY PURPLE VANISH MEADOW ONWARD
Answer: When he started charging people to fish in his creek, it created a—REVENUE STREAM

178. **Jumbles:** TEACUP CRAFTY EXEMPT GOSSIP SMOOTH TANGLE
Answer: After getting in the 10 ITEMS OR LESS line, the customer was ready to—EXPRESS HIMSELF

179. **Jumbles:** GRUMPY NIBBLE PURSER SKETCH FIASCO VIOLET
Answer: He didn't buy the drum set because he wanted—MORE BANG FOR HIS BUCK

180. **Jumbles:** HAPPEN IMMUNE IRONIC GENDER PALACE SLUDGE
Answer: After being served a bagel in first class, the passenger wanted—"PLANE" CREAM CHEESE

187

Need More Jumbles®?

Jumble® Books

More than 175 puzzles each!

Jammin' Jumble®
$9.95 • ISBN: 1-57243-844-4

Java Jumble®
$9.95 • ISBN: 978-1-60078-415-6

Jazzy Jumble®
$9.95 • ISBN: 978-1-57243-962-7

Jet Set Jumble®
$9.95 • ISBN: 978-1-60078-353-1

Joyful Jumble®
$9.95 • ISBN: 978-1-60078-079-0

Juke Joint Jumble®
$9.95 • ISBN: 978-1-60078-295-4

Jumble® at Work
$9.95 • ISBN: 1-57243-147-4

Jumble® Celebration
$9.95 • ISBN: 978-1-60078-134-6

Jumble® Circus
$9.95 • ISBN: 978-1-60078-739-3

Jumble® Exploer
$9.95 • ISBN: 978-1-60078-854-3

Jumble® Explosion
$9.95 • ISBN: 978-1-60078-078-3

Jumble® Fever
$9.95 • ISBN: 1-57243-593-3

Jumble® Fiesta
$9.95 • ISBN: 1-57243-626-3

Jumble® Fun
$9.95 • ISBN: 1-57243-379-5

Jumble® Galaxy
$9.95 • ISBN: 978-1-60078-583-2

Jumble® Genius
$9.95 • ISBN: 1-57243-896-7

Jumble® Getaway
$9.95 • ISBN: 978-1-60078-547-4

Jumble® Grab Bag
$9.95 • ISBN: 1-57243-273-X

Jumble® Jackpot
$9.95 • ISBN: 1-57243-897-5

Jumble® Jailbreak
$9.95 • ISBN: 978-1-62937-002-6

Jumble® Jambalaya
$9.95 • ISBN: 978-1-60078-294-7

Jumble® Jamboree
$9.95 • ISBN: 1-57243-696-4

Jumble® Jitterbug
$9.95 • ISBN: 978-1-60078-584-9

Jumble® Jubilee
$9.95 • ISBN: 1-57243-231-4

Jumble® Juggernaut
$9.95 • ISBN: 978-1-60078-026-4

Jumble® Junction
$9.95 • ISBN: 1-57243-380-9

Jumble® Jungle
$9.95 • ISBN: 978-1-57243-961-0

Jumble® Kingdom
$9.95 • ISBN: 1-62937-079-8

Jumble® Knockout
$9.95 • ISBN: 1-62937-078-1

Jumble® Madness
$9.95 • ISBN: 1-892049-24-4

Jumble® Magic
$9.95 • ISBN: 978-1-60078-795-9

Jumble® Marathon
$9.95 • ISBN: 978-1-60078-944-1

Jumble® Safari
$9.95 • ISBN: 978-1-60078-675-4

Jumble® See & Search
$9.95 • ISBN: 1-57243-549-6

Jumble® See & Search 2
$9.95 • ISBN: 1-57243-734-0

Jumble® Sensation
$9.95 • ISBN: 978-1-60078-548-1

Jumble® Surprise
$9.95 • ISBN: 1-57243-320-5

Jumble® Symphony
$9.95 • ISBN: 978-1-62937-131-3

Jumble® University
$9.95 • ISBN: 978-1-62937-001-9

Jumble® Vacation
$9.95 • ISBN: 978-1-60078-796-6

Jumble® Workout
$9.95 • ISBN: 978-1-60078-943-4

Jumpin' Jumble®
$9.95 • ISBN: 978-1-60078-027-1

Lunar Jumble®
$9.95 • ISBN: 978-1-60078-853-6

Mystic Jumble®
$9.95 • ISBN: 978-1-62937-130-6

Outer Space Jumble®
$9.95 • ISBN: 978-1-60078-416-3

Rainy Day Jumble®
$9.95 • ISBN: 978-1-60078-352-4

Ready, Set, Jumble®
$9.95 • ISBN: 978-1-60078-133-0

Rock 'n' Roll Jumble®
$9.95 • ISBN: 978-1-60078-674-7

Royal Jumble®
$9.95 • ISBN: 978-1-60078-738-6

Sports Jumble®
$9.95 • ISBN: 1-57243-113-X

Summer Fun Jumble®
$9.95 • ISBN: 1-57243-114-8

Travel Jumble®
$9.95 • ISBN: 1-57243-198-9

TV Jumble®
$9.95 • ISBN: 1-57243-461-9

Oversize Jumble® Books

More than 500 puzzles each!

Generous Jumble®
$19.95 • ISBN: 1-57243-385-X

Giant Jumble®
$19.95 • ISBN: 1-57243-349-3

Gigantic Jumble®
$19.95 • ISBN: 1-57243-426-0

Jumbo Jumble®
$19.95 • ISBN: 1-57243-314-0

The Very Best of Jumble® BrainBusters
$19.95 • ISBN: 1-57243-845-2

Jumble® Crosswords™

More than 175 puzzles each!

More Jumble® Crosswords™
$9.95 • ISBN: 1-57243-386-8

Jumble® Crosswords™ Jackpot
$9.95 • ISBN: 1-57243-615-8

Jumble® Crosswords™ Jamboree
$9.95 • ISBN: 1-57243-787-1

Jumble® BrainBusters™

More than 175 puzzles each!

Jumble® BrainBusters™
$9.95 • ISBN: 1-892049-28-7

Jumble® BrainBusters™ II
$9.95 • ISBN: 1-57243-424-4

Jumble® BrainBusters™ III
$9.95 • ISBN: 1-57243-463-5

Jumble® BrainBusters™ IV
$9.95 • ISBN: 1-57243-489-9

Jumble® BrainBusters™ 5
$9.95 • ISBN: 1-57243-548-8

Jumble® BrainBusters™ Bonanza
$9.95 • ISBN: 1-57243-616-6

Boggle™ BrainBusters™
$9.95 • ISBN: 1-57243-592-5

Boggle™ BrainBusters™ 2
$9.95 • ISBN: 1-57243-788-X

Jumble® BrainBusters™ Junior
$9.95 • ISBN: 1-892049-29-5

Jumble® BrainBusters™ Junior II
$9.95 • ISBN: 1-57243-425-2

Fun in the Sun with Jumble® BrainBusters™
$9.95 • ISBN: 1-57243-733-2